# Being Strong

*By Stacey Ann Satchell*

Being Strong
Author: Stacey Ann Satchell
Published by: Stacey Ann Satchell

All rights reserved. No part of this book may be reproduced or transmitted in any form or by any means, electronic or mechanical, including photocopying, recording or by any information storage and retrieval system, without written permission from the author, except for the inclusion of brief quotations in a review.

Copyright © 2013 by Stacey Ann Satchell
First Edition, 2013
Published in USA

Matthew 19:14: But Jesus said, "Let the little children come to me and do not hinder them, for to such belongs the kingdom of heaven.

Psalm 34:18: The Lord is near to the broken hearted and saved the crushed in spirit.

2Corinthians 1:4: Who comforts us in all our afflictions, so that we may be able to comfort those who are in any affliction, with the comfort with which we ourselves are comforted by God.

2Corinthians 4:16-18: So we do not lose heart. Though our outer self is wasted away, our inner self is being renewed day by day. For this light momentary affliction is prepared for us an eternal weight of glory beyond all comparison, as we look not to the things that are seen but to the things that are unseen. For the things that are seen are transient, but the things that are unseen are eternal.

Deuteronomy 3:8: It is the Lord who gives before you. He will be with you; he will not leave you or forsake you. Do not fear or be dismayed.

# Acknowledgements

This book is in honor of my children lives here on earth and during their passing. You will see the never-ending reward of the Lord, the journey in which He had taken me on before, during and after their death. Shayne and Stephaune born March 10, 2000 and September 12, 2009, respectively both died on April 3, 2011. I extend an unending thanksgiving and gratitude to my earth Angels Joy Johnston, Jeanna Harding, Pam, the gentle man who came in person to pay his respect to my boys at their wake and all the others involved in being at the accident scene, there are no words to express my gratitude towards them.

In this book you will understand as you read why they achieve the title they all have. When I first prayed about this book, I waited upon the Lord and my response came and the name 'Being Strong' was birth. I know I would not be able to talk about myself so therefore I have relied upon the universe and encouragement of those who love me to complete this assignment.

You will also see where my motivation was developed and strengthen, scripture say, even out of the mouth of babes, so cheers to my angelic babes of strength.

When I started this book it was never in my deepest imagination that so much growth and people would play a significant role in the completion of this book. Those that I thank before where the ones that was at the beginning of this tremendous journey, from the amazing children to the angelic beings God placed in my life before knowing 'Being Strong' would be my first publish book. Through prayer and supplication and these great people my story comes to life. Thanks to my wonderful daughter Shaniece, my sister Shermika Baynham for creating the cover of this book. A extending thanksgiving to a lady I never met before writing this book, but believe God placed her in my life to give me the courage and understanding to finish up and publish this book; my teacher Judith Curr. My Aunt Reka Cooke for her excellent advice. Thanks for all the love and support of my family, my mother Pansy Satchell, inherited dad Charles Sneed, my brothers Paul and Richard Satchell, Aunts, Uncles, Cousins and children inherited from God. A special thank you to each and everyone that has played a role in my life; the kind words, thoughts, and prayers. Extended thanks, to my Fidelitas sisters for your continuous contribution of prayers and thoughts throughout this journey of my life. Each of you have played an important role in the development and birthing process of 'Being Strong.' Thank You.

# Tribute

When the Lord blessed my womb, He blessed me with Angels. Shayne and Stephaune were two of my blessing. I have never been happier. I cherish every moment I had with my precious children, Shayne and Stephaune. So now, I can have peace for I was present for their first words, steps, teething, sleepless nights, and sickness. Every event in their lives significant or not I was there.

I love Shayne so much, I never even imagine having another because I thought he was all I needed and would ever need. We did everything together. He was my prince, my knight in shining armor, my angel on earth. He was everything to me. I am going to miss his smiles, the way he winked is eyes, the genial look he had when going to do something cheeky, the way his presence lit up a room, his hugs and kisses, he saying, "I love you", and he coming to jump on me. Him climbing into my bed saying, "Mommy I am gonna sleep with you." Watching him walk home from school, all the phone calls and text messages.

I am going to miss waking at night watching my two precious angels sleep. Shayne and Stephaune were a part of a whole but piece-by-piece we will join together once again in the Kingdom of God. I am going to miss running ward at nights, tucking them in at nights, going to the park, pool, just having fun at home or out; and being able to be proud whenever they do something remarkable.

I miss Stephaune mainly because he was like a physical part of me; he was always in my hands and would never allow me to ever put him down. It seem like he knew time was limited. So he didn't want to miss precious times with his mommy. Praise God I was the kind of mom that always want to be in the presence of my boys like they did me. I miss my mammas' boys so much, but I know they are in a better place. Love and miss my Kings, Mammas boys and My Binky Baby. Heaven Bounded April 3, 2011.

# Table of Contents

The Beginning: Where it All Started.................15
My Findings.................................................35
Babe in Christ.............................................45
My Newest Blessing....................................57
Turning Point.............................................77
My Visions Continued.................................85
Turmoil......................................................93
The Journey Begins..................................105
Moment Of Truth.....................................121
The Funeral.............................................133
Life after the Fact....................................143
Part of the Healing Process......................151
The Truth Reaveal...................................175
Almost Complete.....................................183
Closure...................................................195
Bonus Chapter........................................207
About the Author....................................229
Contact..................................................230

# 1

# The Beginning: Where it All Started

It all began when I became pregnant with my daughter, Shaniece in January 2006. Confuse and happy at the same time for I had planned my life around my precious and priceless angel Shayne, who was born March 10, 2000.

Even though I had hopes of having six children, once Shayne was born I became the happiest person to have ever lived.

He was perfect. Everything about my baby boy was just right. He caused me to start thinking on

God and I knew in my heart I was the first woman on earth to have birth an Angel.

It may sound a bit corny but it was every thought in my heart that first day I laid eyes on my precious child, Shayne

Everything about him was perfect. Even though Shayne was is middle name, it was perfect and it was the name I decided on calling him when he got home. Just like my older brother who had our fathers' name; he was call by his middle name to lessen the confusion of calling one name and having two persons showing up at once.

I find myself laughing at the very thought of it all.

Back to my angel… Shayne had perfect fingers, the most adorable eyes, lashes, and brow, anyone could have ever dream of having. If there was a flaw, I didn't see it! Maybe it's because he was my child, but more than that, the feeling of having an angel, in my heart; felt more real every time I saw my precious child.

As he grew, his personality came to life. He was loved and adored by everyone he shared time and space with.

Everyone that knew me at this time in my life thought my vocabulary was slim to none because everything was "and Shayne this, and Shayne that".

Writing about it now is like turning back the hand of time and every bit of it feels so real, like I am reliving it all again.

I sat day in and day out thinking to myself; well this is a blessing, though I didn't want any more children. But the feeling of being torn between two loves is all I felt.

I was excited at the fact that I was having another child but at the same time, I was selfish to my own inner thoughts. For now Shayne will have to share me with my new love.

Three months had pass before I realize and it became more of a reality with each day, I was once again responsible for another precious life.

I sat everyday mixing and matching letters in our names, if it were a girl or if it were a boy? But as I wrote daily 'Sha' from Shayne's name and 'n" to represent my middle name, not yet sure as to what her name would be or even if my unborn child was going to be a girl or not, my heart was hoping for a princess; for I was a lover of girl children all my life, till God bless me with a 'Prince' an 'Angel' that stole my heart.

Now my unborn child was five month and the excitement grew more by the second, with every movement in my tummy. But fear had its glory day in my mind.

What if it's not a girl?

Could I love another baby boy, the way I have love Shayne?

Would everything change?

What was to come with a new baby?

I tried replacing my fears of the, what if's? With it's a girl and her name is going to be Shaniece Alyssa!

Every day I would talk to her, calling her by her names, 'Shaniece' or 'Alyssa,' trying to see which one she would move to the most.

Even though I was more leaning towards Shaniece, for the first letter for both my name and their fathers' name began with 'S,' that was also how Shayne got his middle name.

Six month pregnant now, ready to make arrangements on what to buy, and the decision-making came in play, what color to buy?

Dresses and bows?

Pants shorts and shirts?

What colors?

Pinks? Blues?

I believe unisex colors are better for now!

Maybe I should do only pin under and chimes.

All these thoughts brought me to a dark place, for what reason? I had no clue at the time.

In my room, twisting and turning from an unexplained feeling, I got out of the bed, and went over to the loveseat in my room. Before I knew it, I was on the floor in a praying position, praying and asking the Lord for guidance, and to take this tormented feeling away from me.

That very day as I kneel on the floor, hanging over the love seat, I asked the Lord, "God can you please give me a daughter."

Even though I had asked God for my baby girl, I still didn't feel complete. At this time, I started to feel an emptiness in my womb.

Still not understanding what this new feeling was, but knew I wanted it to, Go!

I look up to the heavens and said, "Lord if you give me a daughter, I promise you this day Lord; I will serve you till the day I die."

To my surprise, I was fill with what I had not known, but that emptiness inside was gone, and my unborn child was kicking like crazy; like she was saying, mommy I am back.

At this time I was all smiles and felt like I could face the world. It was an unusual and unexplainable feeling. It was the best I ever felt since my dad died in a car accident in September 1988.

I wasn't sure what it was or how long it was going to last, but I was enjoying every bit of it, especially because most of my prenatal symptoms where lessoning.

Seven month pregnant at my OBGYN waiting to have a sonogram done. My mind by this time was set on; I am having a girl, for God says so!

This was the crazies' assurance ever to me, and surprising at the same time for I had many spiritual experience throughout my life, but was hell bent on my own way of doing things, I am not ready for God just yet!

It was my favorite quote.

I remember this day like it was yesterday, Shayne and I arrive at the OBGYN. Overly excited I was for I knew within, God has answer my prayers, but at the same time being a mother had to take in consideration what my angel wanted; for he has been an only child for me for over six year and it was important what he wanted too.

We weren't on the same chapter though, for he wanted a little brother, he already has a big sister, by his father.

Once again I was torn between my two loves'.

I wanted my princess and he wanted a brother!

I sat talking to him before going in for my schedule sonogram, for it would hurt more to see my baby unhappy. He was everything to me and his happiness was more important than my needs!

Shayne was so sure and unwilling to accept any result other than a baby brother.

Not enough time to convince him, or to let him become acceptable that, the choice was Gods.

It was my second time being called so it was the moment of truth!

His face lit up like a crystal Christmas light. His dimples sink so deep in and his check plumper than I have ever seen it before.

By this time I was praying. "Lord I know my prayer has already been answered, but please come on in and grant my baby peace, understanding, and joy."

Shayne never took his eyes off the monitor; he sat just below the Diagnostic Medical Monographer, rubbing me in comfort. My angel always felt the need to take care of me.

The moment of truth was here, she asked; "do you want to know the sex?"

With confidence I replied, "I already know."

All smiles I was by this time, glimpsing back and forth at my angel.

She responds, "It's a girl."

I couldn't console my feelings, all giggles and smiles and praises within, which was soon

shorten by his soft voice, "I wanted a brother."
You have to laugh at his sense of humor.

He turned to her and asked, "look again, is there one for me, maybe a brother?"

So thoughtful he was! I knew he was a born angel, from the first day I laid eyes on him.

She smiled and humor him by looking again, showing him the different parts of the baby.

"I want a brother"

"You are going to be a protector for your little sister"

"Yes, but now I have three sisters' and no brother"

"Look how happy mommy is"

"I am happy she is happy, but are you sure there isn't a baby brother in there for me"

I interrupted them, "honey come and touch mommy belly, your sister is saying; hello Shayne"

Giggles, giggles and more giggles

"Mommy I still want a baby brother, okay.

So promise me you will get me one next time."

"Sure honey, let see what God says about that."

"Bye big brother, I know you are going to be a great big brother"

Smiles

"Bye Mommy"

"Bye"

So mommy, persistent as always; "so I am getting my baby brother?"

Laughter's

"No problem honey, but you are going to be a lot older than your baby bro whenever he comes."

"I still want a baby brother, maybe God can make him big quick."

Laughter fill the room

My baby was hilarious.

On our way home, we called dad and the family to share the exciting news. Yeah, I am getting a baby sister." Sarcastic voice. Daddy couldn't convince him but uncle Richie was able to make him laugh. It was like medicine to the sick, he was back on track, and I was happy to see my baby happy again.

Eight months now and school as reopened and Shayne is off to school during the daytime.

I sat at the computer one day and curiosity spark my mind. I wondered what Shaniece mean and where it derives from. To my surprise it was the best knowledge I could ever receive.

Shaniece - 'gift from God'

So happy and thankful by my discovery, I was overjoyed, happy, and convinced, that the feeling I couldn't explain those months ago was God trying to get my attention.

I went on to look up her middle name, which started with the letter 'A', for my older brother middle name is Andrew.

At this time in my life, I was so caught up on the movie 'Charmed' and I so loved Phoebe whose real name is Alyssa, which stand for prissy, proper and prep, and in Hebrew, joy and great happiness, and in Germany, noble kind.

Good enough for me!

So this is the history on how I derive at her name Shaniece Alyssa, and after a revelation like, 'gift from God' I was happy. Her name was perfect.

The day I will never forget, my prayer life with God began; October 13, 2006. At 1:00 a.m. The pain of on and off contractions woke me. I watched the time go by, while pacing back and forth, talking to God as my angel slept.

"Lord give me a sense of direction, on what to do next?"

Looking at the time, can't believe it was only 2:00 a.m., breathe in, in, out as the pain come in and out.

"Okay Lord, what next? For I have to get the children ready for school, get a drive, for I can't drive myself to the hospital in all this pain."

Confuse in whether to sit or stand, and praying the time would just go by, so I could call my OBGYN. Walking over to the other side of the bed, kiss my angel as he slept. Thinking, how bless I am for yet again, God as considered me and blessed my womb.

Only this time it was different, for I knew God has given me exactly what I had asked Him for, that day in the room.

'Someone so special, that would shine in remembrance of Him and His word.'

It was now about 3:30 a.m., so I decided to call their dad, to let him know, I was in pain, and to be distracted so the time would go by faster.

"Morning hun, hope it isn't too early."

"Is everything okay?"

"I am in labor, need some company, to help the time pass."

"So, why didn't you call me before?"

"I was waiting till it was almost time, for you to get up for work."

The conversation continued, it was 5 o'clock in the morning; praise is the Lord. I said bye, and started putting my bag together, while packing a bag for Shayne, for his four to five day sleep over by his aunt. This I already knew, for it was going to be another cesarean.

The pain got more unbearable, for although it was my second time having a child, it was very different with Shayne. This is one of the many reason, I was sure he was a born angel. For without the machines the doctor's use to monitor, heartbeat, and contractions, I wouldn't

know, nor would they have known of my contractions, for I felt nothing.

Six o'clock, made breakfast, school drop off, drove back home, called my doctor, my drive, then sat and wait.

Shayne and I went to my doctor in Fort Lauderdale, he checked me, and then sent me by the hospital across the road, to get check on the machine before heading to the hospital of my choice; for I want both my children to be born at the same hospital.

Little did I know; plans were about to change tremendously!

I called my aunt to come pick up Shayne by the hospital.

He sure was my handbag; I went nowhere without him.

She came and got him, and then I went in for my evaluation.

The tables turned so quickly, by the time I could walk in and give my doctors name, and they could get out the necessary paper works, my head water broke; another first.

"Get her to a room"

"Which room is available?"

"This one"

"Let's go, let's go"

"What's your name?"

"Stacey Ann Satchell"

"Got a few question for you"

"Ok"

The questions went on and on, while they prep me and call my doctor to send over my midwife.

Then their came the questions I so feared from the pain started.

"Who is going to be here with you?"

"How many people do you have coming?"

I replied, "no one"

"I will check back in a few, try calling someone, anyone."

"Okay"

Who was I fooling, I had no one to call, so I called on the one person I know will always answer me.

"Lord, I am here alone as you see, apologies

Lord, thank you for showing up, I need you."

By this time, my midwife and doctor had come to check up on me. My doctor said, "Seeing I was so young and waited so long, he would honor my request of seeing if it was possible to have a natural birth."

"Lord do this for me please, I need to have a natural birth."

Thinking about it now, I don't know why it was so important to me; guess it was the recovery process I feared.

However the journey only got me closer to the Lord.

"Jesus is this going to happen, it's after six and I have not yet dilated."

Phone calls come in from everywhere, England, New York and Jamaica. I was happy to hear everyone's voice, but wishing I could just see my princess face already!

"It's after eleven o'clock Lord, what's next?" Well I am anxious but happy for I wanted her to be born on October 14.

"Okay Lord, it's the fourteenth now so make something happen, Lord"

The doctor came and told me, 'I have to go ahead and do the cesarean.' The expression on my face was so obvious, he said, "I will give you another hour, if nothing, I am going to operate." My eyes wailed with tears.

"Lord, how am I going to do this now?"

As plain as day, I heard a voice say; 'You are not alone my child, for I am with you.'

I stared all around the room, wondering, Lord is that you? I doubt am losing it!

The mid wife came to check on me, and realize the baby was in distress, so she went and get my doctor.

"We are going to have the nurses come in and get you ready for surgery."

Lost for a minute, touching on my tummy, telling her; "hang on honey, hang on, mommy love you." "Paper works are to be signed, and they will take you to the operating room after." The doctor said.

"Okay"

Heading to the operating room, I started talking to God.

'It's me and You now Lord, perfect and healthy, okay; thank You'

My phone rang, the nurse answer, it was my brother and I could hear him giving her a hard time, she kept repeating; she's going in now! Guess he wasn't having it, for she hand me the phone; we spoke for a second.

I saw the lights in the operating room, so bright like I remembered from Shayne. It was time, no turning back!

"Lord just before I go, thank You for being with me through it all, thanks for my gem"

Anxiety kicked in, now I just wanted to know, whom was she going to look like?

How am I going to feel when I see her?

Surgery was over; I was in recovery, "thank You, thank You Lord, and thank You"

My room was ready, they took me to my room, and finally I was going to hold my precious baby girl for the first time.

All I could think about was, how I'm going to feel!

The nurses brought her in, to my amazement as I held her and look down at her; it was like looking in a mirror. I will never forget my way to the Lord, I thought.

I could not get enough of my baby girl, I was tired but couldn't close my eyes; I wanted to look at her every second.

When I woke up, all I could think about was, I need a church home! A small one Lord! I want a family Lord! Show me, the signs Lord; I need guidance!

Since I lost my dad, in a tragic car accident in September 1988, I had found some level of joy, and peace, in my cousin, who later died of cancer in February 1998. My children were my therapy, for all, I had lost, which was, everything in my mind, for my father was my world and my cousin replaced that emptiness, and she was gone too.

When Shayne was born, I had a reason to live again; he was my 'morning.' So with his presence, the day could go on. Then now to top it off, I have got me a special gift from God, Shaniece.

# 2

# My Findings

It was now 2007, my daughter was months old, and I was yet to find a church home. I kept praying and asking God for a sign. He knew my heart, I wanted a small church home, where I can learn and grow, and most importantly, I could inherit a family.

Having my children now, I thought it would all be perfect, but something was missing. I couldn't quite put my finger on what it was.

"Could it be, my hunger for God?"

"Maybe I needed to make some changes"

"What Lord, what?"

I continue growing in prayer, reading a scripture a day; hoping and praying, it was all enough. I started praying in my closet, daily I asked, "Lord, is it because, I have done something?" No answer yet!

It was now Shaniece first birthday, so it was a big celebration; everyone was excited.

'A remarkable milestone'

We celebrated at home, inviting others to come celebrate with her. I was feeling the same deep inside, my inside was toiling and turning, I was in an unusual place once again but spent the time enjoying, every second of my precious children.

By this time, I was growing spiritually, getting visions, and being stirred up inside. Why? I had no clue!

So it was almost a week since my princess birthday, and another celebration was about to happen, that would change my life forever. Little did I know, what's to come!

It was my friends' birthday, the day my journey would all begin; we cooked, and invited friends over. A friend wanted some red bull, so my brother and I headed to the CVS at the corner.

Like any other day, we went in and grab what we needed, but I came out with more than I bought. Let's say, God showed up, and I was excited.

My brother was singing along, like he always would.

"Good night"

"Night"

"Night"

Attracted by my brother singing, the gentleman turned to us and said, "I came in to get battery, for bible study"

We both looked at him attentively, he continued, "Would you both like to visit with us on Sunday?"

Me, "sure"

He then gave us the name, direction and time info of the church.

I ran home in excitement, to share the news with my friend whose birthday it was, "I found a church home"

Wow! I thought to myself, like seriously. I can't believe I lived by a church, and never knew.

This was personal to me, so I prayed over it, like everything else.

"Lord, is this the right church?"

Amazed at my findings, I was informed and in such excitement, I went to my bed, a waiting the next day, that would be Sunday. I can't wait to see, what God as in store for me.

I flew out of my bed, upset at myself, for I had over slept; it was minutes to ten! Blowing a gasket in my head.

"How could this happen?" This was unacceptable!

"Lord, did you allow me to sleep in for a specific reason?"

There was no word to explain, my anger toward myself.

So I turned on the television, to see if I could, tune in to a morning service. Still pondering as to, why?

What happened?

For if you know me, I am generally, up at nights walking through the house, making sure all doors was secured. So I just couldn't understand, why?

"Devil, are you, keeping me distracted from what God as in store for me?"

Browsing in and out on the service on TV, as I prepare breakfast for my children.

"Lord, I am going next week, nothing is going to stop me!"

Still, caught up in my mind, as to the why and what happened. I couldn't accept that it was going to bed late, for that was the norm, for even when I didn't go to bed late; I still had to run ward.

That's my expression of, checking around the house, watching my precious children as they slept.

Yet would still being up at the crack of dawn.

I shared my thought with my friend, for she knew what it all meant to me; because it wasn't a secret I wanted a church home. She gave me encouragement to go, while she would watch and care after the children.

The week had flown by so fast, it was Sunday again, October 28, 2007, the beginning, to the rest of my life.

So I was up and ready for Sunday service. Like I can remember my name, this magical experience is unforgettable and priceless to me.

So it was service time, and the atmosphere was nice and pleasant.

Without any knowledge of what was to come. My world was soon to be shaken up.

As I sat thanking God, from within I asked Him, if all my decisions were in line with His plans for my life.

BAM! I was blown away!

The pastor called out a member, to sing, she was sitting about three rows in front of me.

THIS CAN'T BE REAL!

The blood in my veins where rushing through my body, like water bursting through pipes when a reservoir turn on for the first time.

She turned around, amazed and stunned; she inhabited a spirit I was familiar with.

I couldn't believe it!

There was my sign; I was finally home.

She opened her mouth and started signing, it was like an angel ministering to my spirit. She glowed like a candle in a dark room. By this time, I was convinced more than ever that I was home. This lady looks just like my cousin that had passed away from cancer in 1998.

Was this even possible? I felt so special.

I thought to myself, God must really love me. It never at that time, matter to me, if we would ever get a chance to talk. I was too excited, and could feel that empty place within being slowly filled.

If that wasn't enough, it was time for service to begin.

They usher in the elder, for he was conducting service that Sunday. In this very second, before he came out, I was thinking to myself, so I came and I am not going to hear the pastor deliver! Like really!

"Lord, I hope the word comes forward today?"

He sure delivered a service that Sunday, but the Lord had greater things in store for me.

He walked by from the back and went up to the pulpit.

He turned around…'My Lord!'

This couldn't be - was this even possible?

I knew this very moment how much the Lord loves me.

I was home!

There was no doubt in my heart I was home.

By this time I couldn't take my eyes off him, it was the mighty work of the Lord. I knew that day, when bad things happen not to dwell on it, for God will provide a way for you, me, to deal with it.

Today I say this to you, believe it!

I am now anticipating and analyzing in my mind, how am I going to make both these people apart of my life. I don't want to frighten them by my findings, for it was driving my mind wild. All I could think about, is I am coming back!

NO DOUBT ABOUT IT!

Church was over now, and I couldn't wait to shake hand, and cross words with them. I then started to understand, and be thankful that the pastor didn't preach that Sunday.

Now I was thankful, for missing church the Sunday before.

As he closed out with prayer, I could barely bring myself back down from where I had gone.

Trying to digest my gifts from God, for the Elder of the church, look just like my father.

I was beyond excited to take my children, and everyone I cross path with, to the house of the Lord.

God is a God of great rewards, I was beyond thankful!

# 3

# Babe in Christ

I would go to church every week with a hunger for Gods' word. I had a million and one question for the Elder, who was head of the new membership class.

I had given my life over to God, after visiting for three weeks.

I am one to retain everything in my head, but it was overwhelming for my mind was in overload. I started, writing down my questions sheet and sheet of papers, I just needed to know!

With every day, all I could think about, was is it Friday yet?

Sunday hurry up and come.

My children and I would go bible study on Friday nights, soon than you could imagine, Shayne had taken to the church sisters' older child, while Shaniece was happy for someone her age group, which was her baby boy at this time.

I was, beyond happy at this time in my life. I felt unstoppable, if I might add, nothing nor no one could get to me, for I was in a place where no one could get to me.

It was December 2007, I was baptize, what else could a girl ask for, my thought to myself. I was saved, been appointed, had my children, my home was with peace, joy, and happiness. I had it all, what more could there be?

It was the beginning of a new year, and I was excited, for I lacked nothing.

Every time I went through the door of the church, I was in a place that is unexplainable. I would always say, 'I'm home!'

I would look at the Elder, and felt like my father was with me. Even my mom thought he look so much like my father.

By this time, I would confide in him, with any thoughts or questions I had. I pretty much knew, he thought this was because he had been my teacher, but it was a fulfillment of something, I so longed for, 'A Father.'

Like in the world, wherever the pan a knock I was there. I would not miss anything the church kept. These services were like the cherry on top of my already tasty cake.

Everyone knew everyone by name; it was exactly what I requested of the Lord. In which God went a notch further, by slowly filling that emptiness within that I couldn't seem to ever quite put my finger on.

At this time in my life I was just grateful for all God has given me and was satisfy for I thought, what else? Really, what else could the Lord do to exceed what He had already given me?

It's crazy, how life can throw you some wild ball, when you least expect it. I became so distant from God, in my head, for some things were going on in my life by the summer of 2008.

I tried to sort it all out by myself, which was nothing new to me, for I have always been this person; believing I could do it all on my own.

What I lacked was to realize, I was no longer alone, for God is with me, and He finds pleasure in taking care of me.

As much as I should have known this, my old self was fighting with who God was molding me to be. What a distraction this was.

I did the one thing I knew to do which was pray.

"Lord, why am I feeling this way?"

I prayed, but failed to wait on the Lord to answer me.

"Lord, I have everything, but I can't shake the feeling of there is more."

I had a feeling of something bad to come, but I couldn't quite figure it out just yet.

What that would be was a secret to me.

I started reflecting on my pass, remembering all the visions and dreams I had.

The thought scared me, for what I saw in my pass is nothing I wanted to be in remembrance of.

I saw death and turmoil, no wonder I blocked it all out. My only thought was, to start running for maybe if I try I could change the outcome of my future.

Scared daily, for I thought every decision was becoming too heavy for me to bear, but yet again I failed to lay it down before the Lord.

I was single, saved, a single mother, and lost as to what I should do next for every decisions can affect my children future as well as my own.

The devil was happy with his findings, for by this time I could not get the negative thinking out of my head.

I should walk away from the church, for in every vision from the pass I was always saved except for one and in that one vision I could die but God wasn't ready to give up on me.

I could see the car accident I always saw, but could not tell who was present, but my children's father. He never yet died in any of my visions or dreams, but I was always torn apart for others have died.

I believed all this was tied to my salvation, so I thought to myself, God as great purpose for me so I won't die. So maybe if I step out none of this would ever happen.

It was almost the ending of the year and I was still going to church but I wasn't committing to it like I was a year ago.

With the trials of life and daily activities, I was missing church one and two time, which was my way of trying to save everyone.

Again, just like when I was a child and lost my father and cousin, I thought being strong was holding it all in, and taking care of everyone else except myself.

Little I knew it's impossible to love someone if you not love yourself.

This year was at an end, and going to church was at the bottom of my list. I would still visit, for I couldn't step out completely, no matter how hard I tried. I guess that was God way to make sure I never get lost in my own way.

By the time Christmas was here, I was in for a shift; which would leave me bewildered. My children father was back in my life yet again…sighing.

It was a bittersweet journey and time in my life, his other children were here, I was ecstatic, I can't get enough of children; I love them so much.

That was my weakness, for even if the devil came knocking, as long as he had a child, I would let him in. If I could, I would have had six children, but with cesarean, it's impossible.

Every moment with them was joyful, my world was lit, but there came that feeling of destruction. It was even worst now, for I had to worry about four children.

I started going out again, thinking that it would all go away again. Just like before when I was in the world I was distracted by the lifestyle.

With help, this was easy to achieve, and with every argument and disagreement, it's like my safe haven, to go out. While being out, I was free from dealing with what was at hand.

But to my surprise, I couldn't escape my life; for I have a praying spirit, and that's all it took; for it's an opening for Christ to come on in.

"Lord, what am I to do, how EVER did I get here?"

You know Lord, I was happy with just what I had!

Not hearing from God as fast as I hoped, I turn to the Word of God for guidance, where I was reminded of, His abundant, glory, grace, favor and love.

"Lord, I don't mind doing your will but I fear this feeling I feel. If you love me, don't let this, whatever this is come to pass, for I can't deal with it! If it feels this way Lord, and I don't even know what it is, however will I deal with it when it comes?"

"This is not happening Lord, who am I?"

"Am I a prophet?"

"Talk to me Lord, I need answers, why are You not answering me?"

"Do I have to just trust that, You know what You are doing?"

"It's hard Lord, too hard for me."

I made up my mind to do it the Lords' way, even though I have my doubts.

Next question, "Should I stay with him Lord?"

"How do I get him to go without the children?"

"Lord, am I crazy for wanting and loving his children and not him?"

"Or, is it that I can't love him, for I see the pain that lies ahead."
"Hmmm"

"Lord I think I am going to just cut my loss and go. I can't stand this feeling of uncertainty, am I making the right choice?"

My mind was made up, I was going to leave him, go back to church, but where am I going to find the time. I got even more responsibility now, what have I got myself into?

The news hit me like a tornado, I'm lost for words. What am I going to do now?

Back to all I know to do. Angry at myself, "Lord is this my punishment for not being in church for the New Year's?"

As if things weren't confusing and crazy already, I had to add one more to the list.

Only me I tell you, only me!

Now I was left with more decisions!

At that place of joy once again, mixed with confusion, should I stay? Should I go? Was it a sign from the Lord?

Finally, the Lord answered me, saying 'that's not the way; really Lord? Why didn't I hear Him before, was I too distracted.

"Lord, I am married now, as you see, I called you before I made a decision, but I never hear you answer me, not nice!"

I was now confused and needed a revelation, as to where to go from here. I decided I was going to church for I needed answers, for I have gotten myself in the place I tried so hard to avoid; however did I get here?

Everyone at church was excited to see me, I felt right at home as always, and it was as though I never missed a day. This didn't last too long, with all my new responsibility; I barely had any time for myself, much less going to church. I made a decision to watch services on television, read my bible and pray, praying it would be enough to get me through this new chapter of life.

# 4

# My Newest Blessing

So, now it was time to deal with the news that brought me so much joy and confusion. For this very reason I had made the decision to get married and try one last time.

I was pregnant with Stephaune, who became the reason for who I am, and where I am today in Christ.

All my pregnancy brought something new to my life, Shayne made me slow down and become grateful for he was an angel on earth; my angel.

Shaniece encourage in me a prayer life with God, and brought me to the covenant with Christ; that I will serve Him till I die.

So third times the charm they say, so I was excited to see what was to come with this pregnancy. I wondered, what could top the track record I had, an angel, being saved for I received my gem.

Every day, I would be excited to see what the Lord had in store for this pregnancy. At this time, I knew it would have been a boy again, but did not want a boy for that's how my mom had us. I have an older brother and a baby brother, and seeing we weren't in the best relationship at this time; for she didn't agree with my decisions.

I never had to do a sonogram; I just knew what I was going to be having, a baby boy. But up until the sonogram, I was just excited to be having another child, and wanted to know what was going to happen.

I would talk to him every day, rubbing on my tummy and asking who are you going to be? What are you going to like?

These moments were the best, mom and child bonding before birth.

I would tell my unborn baby everything, you have four siblings, three sisters and a brother; who can't wait for you to get here. I would talk about Shayne, more than any of the other children; for he wanted a brother from he was a baby himself.

Even told the baby the story of how Shayne wanted Shaniece to be his baby brother, and stories of the days Shayne would dress up his sister and laugh saying, mommy look at my baby brother. So he knew even in the womb how important it was for him to have been a boy, for I don't know what Shayne would have done if it were to be any different.

The two youngest weren't too fussy, as to whether he was a boy or girl, but his oldest sister a brother, for she thought there was enough girl already.

Every day was fill with excitement, as to what will happen during and after this pregnancy, for there is always something marvelous.

When my baby started reacting to my voice, I was the happiest woman alive. So it became even more exciting to talk to him each day.

The visions were back, but greater than any vision I had in the pass. It was like watching real live television. I would stretch my hand out, trying to touch what I am seeing; but I couldn't.

I needed answers, so I would pray throughout the day, as to what this was. I was hearing from God as clear as two people standing before each other. It's time to go, time to go, but I would reply, I can't, for I have to provide for my children. He replied, "I am your provider, not your job, nor anyone else."

Weeks went by, I kept pondering on Gods' voice saying, "It's time to go, and you are going to need this time." So I made the decision in my mind, I was going back to church; I am going to find the time!

"Lord after the baby is born, I will go back to church, and stop working."

I had been growing in my relationship with Christ, for I was getting the Word however I could, and with my baby in my womb, I had no other choice.

I know my baby was living in me, but with him in my womb, it was like 'life' living in me; it's unexplainable.

I started to grow more with each day, don't know how, but my relationship with God was reconnected somehow. It was restore and added on to, with some understanding, my faith needed to be encourage, but God had prepared for that too.

I had this customer that had suffered from a stroke and walked limp. He would pass by every day, telling me he like me, and I could do well with a husband. I would say to him, "I am married!" But he would pass every day and say the same thing.

I showed him my ring, to prove to him I was married, it was as though he was blind, for he somehow never see my ring, nor my growing tummy. I started to tune him out whenever he would come up to the store window.

This one day in particular it all started, all I was hearing from God, this man was revealing to me, I was mad at first thinking who tell this man my business.

He said to me the first time, "I am sorry, I am sorry."

I said, "Sorry for what, you haven't done me nothing?"

He continued telling me how sorry he was and I kept on asking why, at this time I was thinking to myself, he must be getting crazy. I have been convicted, he replied.

He finally acknowledge that he was wrong for the way he behave, even after I kept telling him, I am married.

He expressed his regret and explained, that he wasn't hearing me all along.

He continued to tell me it was just a fleshly desire and he is very sorry, and how he should have known better for I am a child of God.

I respond, "But I been telling you this for months, plus I am pregnant, so what did you think?" He then, said sorry a few more time and left.

At that time I was lost for word as to what just happened, that's like one of the craziest thing that ever happen to me. By the nightfall, he came back saying to me, "you know you should listen."

My thought at the time was is this man coming to me with a whack line.

Sigh!

So cheesy!

"God was talking to you the whole time but you weren't listening."

In my mind, this man bright eeeh.

He continued, "I know you know what I am talking about."

I wanted to tell him to leave me alone, but he was right on point. I believe he realize it, for he excused himself and said, "I don't want to upset you, so I will go, but I have some scriptures for you to read; write them down.

I went home and read them, destruction was heading my way, this was my confirmation to get in line; but I needed more time. I was counting down now, more than ever before for my baby to be born; I needed covering.

The man was back the next day, "did you read the scriptures?"

"Yes I did"

"Do you mind if I pray for you?"

"No prob, I never refuse prayer."

He prayed with me and then said he would be back.

My visions were increasing and I kept asking for more time. Calculating all my expenses, I thought to myself, I could work for another couple weeks then leave the job. This was me misunderstanding God saying, 'GO.' I thought it was the job, for I was selling cigarette and alcohol, but it was greater.

So the baby was born, September 12, 2009, just as gorgeous and glowing as Shayne was, I stared at him in amazement; could it be possible.

"God is this even possible, can one person birth two angel."

Thinking back at my prayer to God, I am surprised I never put two and two together.

How could I not see that Stephaune was born for a reason, and that was to take me back to Christ?

Everyone who saw Stephaune thought there was something different and special about him, they just weren't sure what it was, but it was something.

He was home and the children were happy for their baby brother. Every time I saw him and Shayne together it was unsettling; they were perfect. Happy as a mother, but couldn't help to wonder why they glowed.

Even today when I look back at their pictures, that glow is still there.

I ask myself, why didn't you know?

It was obvious, but I know now it was all part of Gods' master plan to get me through losing them.

Six week later and I was back at work, for I had a plan, but God had a plan of His own.

I did keep my promise of going back to church.

I made the request when I went back to work, to not work on Sundays, for I had to go to church.

On Sundays my five children and I were in church. Everyone was excited to see us when we returned to church.

I started filling my elder in on all I had been through, even the man that would show up at the store, telling me what God says, and our daily reading of the bible.

He was happy to see that though I wasn't in church, I was getting the Word.

So the man came up to the store window and said, "What are you doing here?"

I replied, "What"

"Why are you here?"

"I am working"

"Yea, I see"

In my mind, I was thinking this must be the after, for there was always something after the birth.

"God says, you are very stubborn"

"What"

"You heard me"

Laughing hard for I knew not what to say, for I have been going back and forth with God about going back to work.

God said, He told you to go and you are still here. He wanted to know why I found it so hard to conform to Gods' way. I baffled, trying to find a suitable answer, but there was none. He then looked at me and said, "You are taking time out of your time."

He caught my attention; I am taking time out of my time. It was prayer time, for I needed to know what is happening.

It was joy to share all my experience with my elder; I was always so excited to get to church, just for our conversations. I remember one day in particular he turned to me and said, "Sister Stacey, I think you got an angel." I thought so too! I responded.

Still caught up on time out of your time, what did it mean?

It wasn't time for me to know, it was a part of the puzzle, a part of Gods' divine plan. There were more days like this it had become a routine.

Standing at the register, I felt someone come up to the window to my right, before I could say anything. "Do you know they are hiring at IHOP?"

"Don't you see me working?"

"You got to go"

Those words you got to go sparked my curiosity.

Do you know God? The gentleman responded.

"Yes I do"

He looked me in the eyes and said, "Really know God?"

"I have been through so much and every step of the way, even when I didn't acknowledge or ask of Him, God has been with me. The miracles I have received perceive man's understanding. God, and I we have a relationship. I don't just know of God, I know Him!"

The gentleman smiles at me as if he was pleased with my respond; it was as if he got me to realize something; so his job was done.

As sure as I know that I am a girl; that man disappeared in front of me. I pulled the door, ran around the store, for he was just standing in the window; and he is gone. I even search behind the dumpster outside the store.

I started reflecting on what had happen and what was said. I felt it, it's as though God wanted to keep me in remembrance of all He have done, so I would have a track record of His works. The thing I couldn't get over was, 'you got to go.' What was that about? Was it a sign to leave this job or was it a sign to stop working? Not sure yet, so I kept going.

At church and as usual we had to have our chat. I told the elder of what had happen; we were still on the topic I got angels; God's doing a new thing for me. I believed it for there was no other explanation.

"Sis I love you, I truly do."

"I love you too elder, but not as a brother as a father.

Finally I said it; I was relieved to share this with him and everyone else. I shared with him that day in church when I saw him for the first time, how much he looked like my dad, and the death of my father, my cousin, and my first experience of coming to the church. He finally realizes why I kept coming to him with everything; I was happy and so was he.

It was a relief and I was now able to share the whole story with Shermika, it was only fair. She was a part of my life for Shayne was with her every chance she could have him after church.

I was side tracked for a moment, with the joy of being able to share with Charles and Shermika, what they meant to me. Our relationship escalated so fast, I was thankful more with each day; I was now referring to him as my dad.

Know this, every time you snatch up your share of joy, look out!

For the enemy is coming to steal and destroy.

Problems at home got intense, but I was able to subdue it by this time, for I had grown spiritual, and I had spiritual family to help in keeping me covered and grounded.

I could face the world!

So back at work and there he was again, coming up to me once again, "you not leaving?"

"Yes, yes, yes!"

"When?"

"What?"

"It is time to go."

"Keep covered, ok."

I was stubborn, yes I was, so God had to finally step in.

A few weeks later, I took my children to their doctor appointment. Time was running out on me, due to unexpected test, which had to be done. So by the time I got finish with it all, I was running a bit late for work.

Got to work a half hour late, the owner was covering the morning shift, he was rude and disrespectful in the way in which he spoke to me. I quit that day, for I had never been late before and the fact remains, my children comes first, which I also let him become aware of.

That job was not my provider, it was a means to an end, and so I left with no regret.

That evening, when the children got home and saw me, they were so happy. I took that second to reflect on, how deprive I was of time with my children. The best decision of my life, was made in a second, but will last me a lifetime.

Still lost as to what, it's time to go meant.

Being home, it became a reality, I had miss out on a lot. For when I see them in the mornings, that was it. Homework help was done over the phone, and by the time I got home, they were all asleep. All I could do was pray over them and kiss them, which sometimes I was too tired to perform.

Looking at my new angel, I decided to stay home and take care of him. He deserved it, for Shayne, Shaniece, and Abigail even Olivia got that bonding time.

Stephaune was now five month old, and I had only spent the first six weeks with him, for from mid-day every day after I was away at work and not home till eight o'clock; so we needed more bonding time. I sure did enjoy every minute of our bonding.

By the time he turned eight month, I started thinking to myself, maybe I could go back to work again. No door would open for me, so I decided to trust God. This was very hard for me to do, for I love being able to get my children nice things.

God was working it all out, for my better good.

Seeing that every avenue I tried the path was block, I was more now than ever convince that, it's time to go, meant time with my children; so I made a plan to turn my time and attention toward God and my children.

I won't move until God says so!

Having no clue as to where this all will lead, but was willing to put my last buck on God. So with every day I enjoyed my beautiful children, with an aim of not letting the devil distract me from what God as set before me.

Sure as the sun and moon exists that was my plan, but that wasn't what happened. The devil decided to come at me full force; it was crazy;

though I couldn't understand it at first I was soon to realize. God had set up a trap for the devil, yes He did. The more the trials and tribulations came, I turned to the Word of God; the devil was mad.

Things that never happened before started. I know nothing else but prayer, so prayer it was, so I prayed. My best friend mister boom box was on all day playing softly, music or recorded services. This is what got me through it all!

At this time my friend Neisha was pregnant, and I knew for sure my baby boy was special, and uniquely different. Stephaune would communicate with her unborn child in a way you would have to see to believe. For instant, he would let her know when the baby needed to be rub and how to rub the baby.

She be sitting in the kitchen or living area and he would come and set her hand the right way, for there where three positions. Then he would rub it for a moment with her, so she could get a hang of the how, then he would go. If she was to ever stop or change from the way he showed her, he would come charging from where ever he was and take her hand, beat her on it, then set it back the way it was to be, push up his lips and walk away with an attitude. I told you, you would have to see it to believe it, never have I seen anything like this.

The next thing he would do is go before her on his knees whenever she gets up to walk.

Creeping fast as if she was running him down, then he would stop, flip over on his back just beneath her tummy dying with laughter. Always looking at her tummy never at her, and you never had to check her tummy for movement; it was visibly jumping.

By this time Shayne was well grown and measuring on me every minute. He was a precious soul that I never took any credit for. I would always tell everyone it is God who made him that way. He was respectful, loving, caring and sweet in an angelic way; he was different.

Still faithfully going to church, seeking direction as to the what, how to do? I was happy and encourage by growth, especially based on my circumstances.

So it was September 12, 2010, my baby boy was celebrating his first birthday, which at this time I had no clue; it would be is only. Family and friends came to celebrate the milestone of my babies' life. He was so happy, smiling, giggling and playing around; everyone enjoyed him and so did he. He had a full day, my thought as I watch him slept, I was already imagining next year birthday.

Now when I look back at his actions, once again I can't but say he was an angel and he knew it. For he had so much fun that day, going from one hand to the next making himself memorable, like he was building a memory we all would not forget.

# 5

# Turning Point

It was December 9, 2010, and I had started this screenwriting class, which is where the gear shifts. So it was the first day of class and we were told to choose a movie. The lesson was to choose the person that reflects who you are, then watch the movie.

Thinking to myself, I have not done anything like this before, but I am always willing to try. The movie I chose was, 'Secret Life of Bee.'

So back to class again and I was asked to explain why I first chose that movie and why that character. I was elated by my findings, never had I imagine that a simple test like this, can reveal so much about oneself. I was moved and interested to learn and know more.

We then went on to writing poem. It began!

It was collected then distributed back to the class, so now someone else was going to read aloud what was written.

A little scared, for I hide everything. Even something as simple as, what my favorite food, color is, was a secret; it was my thing and no one had to know.

So moment of truth, the first poem was read and the question was asked, "Who do you believe wrote that poem?" To my surprise we were mostly stranger but surprisingly spending a couple minutes around a person, and you could tell who wrote which poem.

Wow! My thoughts.

So writing was a big part of the class, and through my poems and story writing; I was born again. I couldn't believe it, not one bit. The greatest part of this was looking back at my first work to my last. I could see my growth as I read back all I had written. I was growing in faith, understanding, patience, and so much more; the list is long.

This new knowledge made me happy and proud of who I was, growing spiritual more with each day.

At this time, I was also praying in church, my voice was the first of every service on Sunday; intercessory prayer was my position in church. I was being bumped up, my way of saying; I was growing rapidly in Christ.

So cliché, I was saying this so often. There wasn't a day that I didn't acknowledge my growth; God was bumping me up, why?

I had no idea!

It must be great is all I had to say about my speedy growth. I embraced it all, for I was happy with the work of The Lord.

Just before Christmas, I woke up and felt like I shouldn't go to church. The Lord was telling me to rest, but I knew of my responsibility at church so I tried pushing myself. As hard as I pushed myself to go, it wasn't happening; it was useless to try. So I called Shermika and told her my feeling and my thought to come anyhow. She encourage me to stay and do as the Lord says, I trust her so I decided it was best to rest.

My children were asleep, so I went to their empty room and changed the disc, decided that I could worship, pray, and then rest.

As I sang and glorify God, I felt the Holy Spirit fall upon me. The radio stopped playing, but I let it stay for I was in a place I couldn't come from. Speaking in tongue in an unstoppable manner, I was rejoicing in my soul.

The voice of the Lord was plain; we spoke directly to each other.

Writing it all down so I won't forget what He said. He gave me utterance to write books, He gave to me the name 'Tapping into Your Inheritance through Faith.' Thinking to myself, this is big Lord! The thoughts of how this was a big shoe to fill, flooded my mind, why was the Lord bumping me up?

The question at this time was, Lord what do I have to go through to do this?

Why me?

Am I equipped enough?

He wasn't finish just yet, He started revealing what He desires of me to write, whom to go to in order to achieve His will.

So it was bible study that Friday, Shermika came to get me and I started revealing to her what God has done, and that I was to come to her. She was sure God sent me, for she had written down something about faith that God had given her.

All giggles in bible study, so not us! We were like two school children.

It was chosen by the Lord, I was going to be an Author. Still trying to wrap my mind around this idea, for I never saw myself as an author. He also gave me the instruction, to the next book He would have me write, it was big!

Even in the excitement, it kept piercing my heart as to why God was bumping me up so fast. It was like growing from birth to forty in months.

Joking about it was my way of dealing with the knowledge of something BIG is going to happen.

It was enough to cause grief, anger, hatred, and bitterness, something, which was becoming more foreordained with each day.

Woken by a nightmare, I started searching for my children.

Counting…

They were all there; praise is the Lord. Going through the house, making sure all is well then to the bathroom to pray. "Lord, what was that?"

"I can't live with that!"

Thinking to myself, could something so horrid ever be a reality.

Expressing to the Lord I couldn't live.

There is no way, no way!

Lost in my thoughts as to what to do, to prevent my vision from becoming a reality. My visions were becoming clearer, and more frightening. One I could see clear and feel the true pain of, it was bad! More horrifying than the visions I had over the years. This grief was heavier than the pain from the accident I had visions of for years. What am I going to do?

Back to what I know best but with reinforcement this time. I shared with Shermika, I had a vision but won't say what it is, for it can't be manifested but I need prayer. Spiritual warfare kind of prayer, which I learnt about from the books she gave me to read.

She listen to me rumbling on and on, as to how much I need prayer for this was big! She reassured me she is on it. Nothing to express my appreciation, for I got prayer warriors' on my side now, the devil can't win!

So with all this in mind, I also had to think about Christmas, so cheer face on. My children depend on me, so I had to pull myself together.

So Christmas was here and as usual we prepared prayer request for God. Miracles where already in the air, for I had told my children that this Christmas was going to be different, for I had no money to get them anything but God was ahead of me. They received gifts from a church sister at church and more was delivered that Sunday evening.

That was a good way to end the year, my children were taken care of, I was filled with the

Holy Spirit and my children being happy was a dream come through.

# 6

# My Visions Continued

So my visions continued, it was unbearable, for death has a face and it was closer than I want it to be. I kept praying against it, with help from those who knew of my circumstances. That place of emptiness, cause me to feel helpless; there was nothing I could do for it was inevitable. Redirecting my prayer, asking the Lord to please let it be something I could live with. If they had to go, I needed it to be something I could live with, not something that would destroy me. Waiting on the Lord to respond but there was none. So I suggested to myself, He was working it out.

So changing my focus was the plan, fear of my loss aside and all focus on my books that God had given unto me, and enjoying my precious children.

Stephaune was opening up to other people, with his eyes on me always. It was a start, and I loved his personality.

Burning deep within was the look in his eyes, every time I looked at him it was void, I had no idea as to why; but enjoying him was somehow more important.

As I watch him sleep at nights, I couldn't help but reflect on why this emptiness existed when I was happy. The joy of the Lord was in me and I had so many aspirations toward his future, which I couldn't quite seem to grab hold of.

Shayne was glowing more with each day, watching him while he played outside, trying to somehow figure out why he looked so distant from me, but couldn't quite put my finger on it. Now reflecting on it all, I say at times I should have known. From the dreams, visions, and the unusual series of events that took place throughout that time in my life; but truth is it wasn't for me to know.

By this time, Shayne had transform into a child I no longer recognize. He had developed such a zest for life, yet he still lacks the ability to dream. I would ask him, what he hope to become in life, and he would shook his shoulder as though it wasn't important; for it wasn't necessary for his life. At times my patience would be through the roof, but I would replace it with, he still has time for he is still young.

So I couldn't hold my thoughts in no more, so I had to say it, for I never could understand why he looked the way he did. Turning to my friend Neisha, I express my feelings of how Shayne seem to be holding on to life.

Shayne always acted like it was his last day I needed answers. We tossed ideas back and forth, but I sum it up the same was I have done in my mind so many times before. I guess he is finally being a child!

Shayne always act as though he was responsible for taking care of me. So I would justify his actions by thinking, he has now just realized that, he is a child and is enjoying his finding.

It all became a reality, for he was now acting the same way in school, which worried me the more. Even his teacher realizes there was a change in him and his view on life was as though it was limited to him. I then express my views on his behavior, he was being a child for the first, this way she could understand his behavior. Little did I know he was just creating a time capsule, so others would remember him when he was gone?

Shayne was such a fun loving child, who at one time had so much dreams and aspiration. He wanted at the age of three to be the first black president in America. Even at the tender age of three, he knew that it was going to happen one day but he wanted it to be him.

As election news went on of the possibility of a black president, my baby was positive. While daily news asks all the questions, is he going to win?

Does he have a chance?

My baby nine at the time was confident in the fulfillment of his vision. Shayne would make expressions such as; "Obama is the president of

America," even though it had not become a reality yet. Mommy, I told you America was going to have a black president, he said it over the years, so he was just confirming his word. He would express his love for Obama and ask why bother have an election he is the president. I would smile with delight for his confidence. Moved by his proclamation, for he said it at three years old and seven years later it's becoming a reality. Now you see why I couldn't understand, how such a dreamer could have no dream.

So often, I would remind him of things he had hope for as a child, but he was so sure he wasn't going to need none of this.

Did he know his life was limited?

I will never know the answer but all his behavior says yes!

My next step was to find the next best thing to give him an adrenaline for life, for I had so many dreams for his future. Sunday school was my idea; if he gets an understanding of the word then he can hear from God and be directed from his thoughts of I am not going to need none of this!

Not the best option; for it wasn't how I imagine it would have been. Shayne would rush through the scriptures, memories the verses, and answer the questions in seconds, with a focus to go outside to see his friends.

The look in his eyes would talk to my heart, mommy let me go, you got to let me go play with my friends, for I don't have much time.

This would scare me white!

Trying to slow him down and throw off the words I hear coming from his eyes; I would say, "Shayne you need to understand what you read, don't just read to get it done, but read with understanding."

His reply would blow me away each time.

"Mommy I already know God"

"God never change mommy"

"Mommy, mommy, you know God loves us"

"Mommy God is the way, follow Him and we will be okay"

"Everything in the bible is the same mommy, God giving us instruction"

This would shake me up every time and I would just say, "go play, just make sure I can always see you."

He would be so grateful expressing himself by saying I love you, the words from his mouth that translate in my mind as, mommy you are the best but I got to go, I don't have much time.

Lost in a stair as I watch him play from the patio, wishing I could just reach him for he is so far away.

This dissect my inside every time, it's so strange with all that was visible to me, yet I fail to see, I guess it wasn't Gods' intended plan for me to understand just yet.

Always feeling the need to keep them close to me grew more with each day. There was a routine; Shayne would go off to school in the mornings with Abigail, while Shaniece and Stephaune would be home with me all day. Stephaune would nap by noon and whenever he was awake before school out, we would all go to the gate to meet Shayne and Abigail.

Otherwise they would come in and once Stephaune wakes; we would go to the park across the road. Shayne so enjoyed these time together, he would so look forward to us going to the park or walking around the complex where we lived.

I would watch them as they slept at night. Sometimes Shayne would just jump out of his sleep saying, "Mommy you scared me." He never understood, but that was "my perfect". They all came from me but they all looked so different, yet the same.

With all my planning, I would be so confident it was all going to work out, and 2011 was going to be our year; but little did I know I was up for a challenge so big.

# 7

# Turmoil

So things took a turn for the worst, at this time I thought it couldn't get any worst. The turmoil in the house was becoming unbearable, more for my children than myself. Which drove me to a place of darkness, could this be Lord?

I was lost for words! I start covering my children and myself in prayer, for the first, my latest vision seem like it's about to become a reality. I spent every day making peace with God, securing our place with the Lord. My thoughts, if it's going to happen, we are all going to the Lord.

Shaking myself back to reality, am I serious?

Why am I so willing to die?

I was going to fight to the end!

Giving up wasn't an option, nor was it going to be my reality.

Creating a game plan in my head to separate my children, for it would be impossible to run with four children. My thought was to get the girls secure first, for they are girls. So I made arrangements to get them out the house, so they could be safe, holding on to my boys for dear life! Believing within, as long as they are with me, they will be okay; no harm can come unto them, for I will keep them covered spiritually and physically.

So the girls were out the house and it was my boys, God, and I. Those around me who knew of my situation kept encouraging me to give up the baby and run with Shayne, but I couldn't he was my baby and would be safe as long as he was with me.

The whirlwind had landed; I had to be fighting for my children. A day I never had imagine, so I had to create new routines and a system with Shayne on the days I had to be at the courthouse. Is safety was my priority, Stephaune was always with me, so I never had to worry about him.

Coming from the courthouse, rushing to get home to grab Shayne from the clubhouse. Got to the complex and I didn't see him, I felt death upon my shoulders, I was so heavy physically. I storm throughout the community, a sigh of relieve, and I found my baby.

Trying to pull it all together, for I couldn't allow my baby to see fear in my eyes. It wasn't happening, he saw it and was upset that he made me worry. Reassuring him I am okay and all was well, and for him to not worry about me.

There came a blow I can't understand, even till this day. The words came from his mouth, my heart sank so deep, and I thought life left my body for a moment.

"Mommy"

"Yes Shayne"

"I don't want you to die"

Tears in my eyes, but with all I have within me I held them back, looked my baby in his eyes while holding is cheeks in the palm of my hand.

"Shayne nothing will happen to mommy, God isn't ready for me yet."

It got worst, my whole world began to spin as my baby looked at me and said, "Mommy, I rather if I die." Lost as to what to do or say, I gathered my words and said to him, "Shayne, don't say that!"

By this time, the control was no longer mine. With tears streaming down my face and my voice trembling I said, "Shayne don't say that!"

He looked me in the eyes and said, "But mommy, I don't mind going, I want you to stay alive, they are going to need you." Crying

"Shayne, Shayne, look at me."

Looking deep into his eyes I said, "Honey, there is no life without you, you are my morning, and there can't be a day if the morning never comes."

My baby was still taking care of me, "Mommy, you will be okay, I know it!"

Tears falling on my chest, I wiped his eyes and then mine.

"Don't you worry about anything, I am going to take care of everything, I promise!"

It was my two boys and me and I had to be their rock, I had no choice but to take my place in protecting them.

That night while they slept, I was in the most excruciating pain ever, I did everything to suppress my pain, but couldn't. I started asking God to heal me, for He knew I can't afford to go to the hospital, I have my children to care for.

Starting to think, what could be causing this pain? I went on the internet to find answers, for this was about the second time I felt such pain, pain that cause me to feel as though all my organs were being torn down on the inside.

Missing my girls at the same time, praying my boys survive the storm ahead, was all I could think about. Every day as life kept going, despite the obstacles being packed up in front of me, I kept focus on… I am going to overcome this.

There wasn't a day I didn't ask God to keep us cover and for confirmation that what I was doing was the right thing to do.

With all that was going on, I had to figure a way out for us. The lease was up, so we had to move, not that I mind for then I could sleep knowing we are safe from the physical fear I had. Getting Shayne transfer to a new school, something I normally wouldn't be happy about, but he was going back to his elementary school where he did first and second grade, so I found comfort in, the change won't be a bad one.

More importantly Shayne birthday was coming up, and I had to find a way to make it special and memorable. Not that I had a choice, for he was counting down to his birthday before the month even started. Calculating my birthday, age, and how tall he was getting. I will never forget our birthday; it was our last one together.

It was a week or more before his birthday and he sat at the dinner table with his brother, he turned to me and said, "Mommy, what do you do in the bathroom?

I replied, "I go there to talk to God."

He looked over at me in the kitchen, with a look of acceptance.

"Mommy, what's that language you speak in?" "The language of God honey."

"Oh"

Looking at me now, with curiosity, "is that the same thing like aunty Shermika does at church?"

"Yes Hun"

"But you both sound a little different." Laughter fills the room.

I then looked over at him, and their go that squint in his eyes. He excuse himself, and I couldn't stop giggling, for I could see I had sparked a curiosity in my son, something I so longing to see. He was excited about something and wanted to know more.

Finishing up dinner while playing with Stephaune, Shayne entered from my bedroom into the dining area. The look in his eyes was rewarding to my soul, I was happy, my baby was curious about something.

He sat at the dining table, looked over at me in the kitchen, "Mommy, guess what?"

"Yes honey"

"I spoke to God"

Laughter filled the room again

I looked over at him and smile, I guess he realize I was humoring him.

"Mommy, seriously," with a giggle in is voice. "And you know what? He answered me."

"Okay honey"

"He said, next time He will really talk to me but it be different"

Shayne couldn't contain himself from giggling, "For real mommy!"

"Okay, God is going to talk to you."

Dinner was served and we all prayed, ate, and then off to some television before bed. As with every night, I watched them sleep for a while before going to bed myself.

So my birthday was here and as usual Shayne remembered. He wished me a happy birthday, got ready for school and was through the doors. That day I looked at Stephaune, for unlike usual, it was just he and I for the day for Shaniece wasn't there. He didn't even recognize it was my birthday, but time spent with him was always pleasurable.

School was over and Shayne came rushing through the door. He rushed to hug me and I lift him up, and then back down. Stephaune was asleep, so I told him to get his homework done, and then he could have some playtime. For the first he wasn't overly excited to go play, he wanted to spend time with me, I was excited but in pain at the same time.

The rain poured that night and the boys went to bed early. Sigh of relieve for me, because the pain was back. I now started reflecting on the other times I felt like this. Now am convince it wasn't sickness, it was lifting Shayne. So I passed it off as, my body can't tolerate heavy lifting.

Twisting and turning in the chaise, praying the pain would just go away. About two hours now and the pain keeps elevating, by then Shayne had missed me from the bed, and came looking. Playing it all cool I headed into the room with him and went to bed.

Two day later and it was Shayne birthday, he was excited to go to school. Packing up to go, with Stephaune asleep and Shayne at school, I got the ball rolling. By the time he got home, the truck was all packed, and it was time to go. So worried about is friend, he wanted to say goodbye. He spent a couple hours with them while I make sure everything was done.

Ready to leave!

Shayne was in tears for he was going to miss his friends and school, or did he know it was his final goodbye?

It was the second Sunday in March and I woke up without my boys in my bed, and the girls were with family. The house felt like ghost town, quiet as ever. Headed to the bathroom to pray and have a serious talk with the Lord, for this had to change, how was I to function without my children around.

Got ready and went to church, Sunday school was over and it was time for service. I went to the front of the church like every other Sunday, energized and ready to pray.

"Hallelujah"

Is all I could say, I was feeling a weight upon me, tried to pull myself together but I couldn't, my voice got lower and lower and my head bow down. I felt a hand behind me, next thing I knew I was down on the floor crying like there was no tomorrow. For some reason, I couldn't stop crying, it was an overwhelming feeling of loss, and I couldn't help but cry. Eventually I got up and went to sit in a chair, trying to contain myself and make some sense of what I was feeling.

Church was over and Shermika asked, "What was that about sis?" I told her I felt like I had loss my boys. She reassured me, by telling me that it's because am not use to them not being around and my phone would soon ring.

It sure did, it's like he heard her.

"Mommy"

Smiles across my face, it was my baby.

"Church over? I was watching the time to call you."

"It just did."

"Stephaune is okay, I am taking care of him.

Shayne so knew how to make me happy. We spoke on and off throughout the whole day. Eventually I had to put my phone on vibrate, for everyone was watching television. There was no limit to our communication, when we weren't talking; we were sending text and he would be sending me pictures of him and Stephaune. The love and connection we shared was one of a kind.

# 8

# The Journey Begins

Finally settled into our new home and its time for my babies to once again get adjusted to a new. They were both happy and that's all that is important to me. Planning what's next, for I couldn't keep doing this, they said twelve weeks visitation on weekends, but that was too long for me. As always I turned to God, making a list of all my requirements to happiness.

Shayne was still feeling that traveling pain through is body. The doctor said, all was well, but my mother instinct didn't agree. It was something; I just couldn't quite put my finger on the what. Putting my positive hat on, I encouraged myself; it's all going to be okay.

It was March 22, 2011, on our way to get Shayne registered in school. On the phone with my mom looking at Shayne as he walked in front me. It was the most unusual thing ever, he was close enough for me to touch him, but looked as though he was half mile ahead of me. I shook the feeling off, and counted it as nothing.

Acting shy for a minute, then decided it was okay, he would go to his class alone. We exchanged hugs and kisses and he said, I will call you when am on my way home. Stephaune and I then headed home, to have our time. We had a fun day as expected; he went down for his nap at midday as usual.

It was 2 p.m. and my phone rang, it was Shayne, letting me know he was on his way home. Looking at the time, I was excited, my baby be home in a couple minutes. The phone rang again, "Mommy, how I don't see you?"

"Stephaune is still asleep Hun, I am looking through the window."

Shayne was so use to our routines, he expected me to be standing at the gate or making my way toward him.

I saw him coming and said to him, "I see you."

"I don't see you mom."

"Look to your right."

"I see you," in his giggling, voice.

I ran to the door before he could walk up. Hugs and kisses were exchange and he was happy to see his brother.

He started telling me everything about school; he was excited in a way I haven't seen in a while. I was happy for the first in a long time, I saw dream in my baby's eyes, and he was so looking toward going to school the next day. We had church that night, so we got some rest.

It was church time and this lady kept looking in, she requested prayer and they prayed for her. Standing in the hall, trying to calm down Stephaune, she passed by on her way home. She stretched her arms out and he went to her. Shermika mouth fell, for that was a first!

Stephaune hug that lady like he had known her. She soon started speaking in tongues and breaking down. Turning to me she says, "I feel pain, hurt, it feels familiar." I smiled at her, but never doubt her feelings, for when she had received prayer they said she was a future prophet; and I also had the same feelings. It was obvious; she was growing in her gift, she just couldn't be sure of her foreseeing for it wasn't clear. Maybe it was for the best!

It was Friday and Shayne was off to school, anxiously awaiting is arrival home, for I knew there was going to be more stories. My joy lies in my children, everything they do was something significant to me.

That evening we were to go on the road, instead we ended up at Checkers for dinner. It was our last meal, Shayne made that dinner date happen.

We went to meet up with Neisha for I was babysitting for her. We went to the CVS to get some things for Stephaune and Shaniece. He wouldn't stop till Neisha gave him her undivided attention, for he wanted her to remember, what it is that her son is going to need.

Shayne was so sure he knew what Amarii was going to need. He would keep repeating and showing her over and over again. He even had to show me because he wanted me to remind her.

Did he know it was his last days?

Heading through the store door, he turn to me, "Mommy, let's go to Checkers"

"Shayne, I have something else to do."

"But mommy, it be like old time."

He captured my heart that very minute, "Okay honey." He was excited!

My heart was fill, my baby was pleased, those words, it be like old time, just weaken my heart. Me, him, Shaniece, and Neisha use to have loads of Checker days.

He order that night, like he knew it was his last meal, he ordered for Stephaune too. We sat ate and I was pleased looking at my boys.

We went home that night and talk for a few before bed, I remember it like it was yesterday.

It was a new day and it didn't start off good. Shayne woke up complaining of his foot bottom hurting.

"Mommy, my foot bottom is tender, it hurt."

"Let's see."

"Its tender mom, you know like when you been traveling along time."

Looking at his feet, I saw no imprint; I was puzzled and decided to do what I know best, pray. He kept trying to convince me, it was there but I couldn't see anything. As I covered him with the sheet, I wonder, what could this be?

I prayed over him and told him to rest until his feet felt better.

Sometime had pass and he said it was better, but I felt like he only said so because he wanted me to feel better? I sent him to go get ready while I call aunty to make arrangement for their drop off.

Still at the end of the bed playing with Stephaune, I felt this emptiness of missing him. He started kissing me, that thing that was to be sweet, scared me. Stephaune was that child you couldn't kiss; he would slap you or walk away. So I push him off, but he came back again and again. I held him by both arms and said; "Stephaune don't do that, mommy isn't going to die."

He giggled so hard, I wonder if he understood me. That didn't stop him however, for he kept on kissing me. Guess he was saying good-bye!

Tickling him, the room was fill with giggles. I remember it so clearly. He started talking; I had to stop, for my baby sounded like me when I am in spirit.

"Stephaune, mommy has the gift of translation but I don't know how to do so yet."

We both looked at each other and burst out in laughter. The look in his eyes was like he understood me at that moment. I finally took the opportunity to kiss him. Stephaune was that child that never had to do nothing; you just had to love him.

Shayne came from the bathroom to get dress, again I ask, are you sure you are all right?

"Yes mommy," he responded.

That was just to make me feel better! For at the last minute, he never wanted to go. I promised him it would be his last visit, for I was going back to court, to ensure they never had to go back.

He sat putting on his shoe and as the person we stayed with came to say bye, I turned to her and said, "You have to come and say bye, for you won't see him again."

Without knowledge of what I really said, hugs and good-bye were exchange, and we then finish up to leave.

As we walked it was more visible, Shayne never wanted to go, but he wouldn't admit it. He was still taking care of me!

We got there and it was now Stephaune turn, he started hanging to me for dear life. Aunty took him and insist I just go, he be all right. Stephaune was still crying, I kissed him and left.

Walking up the road, I stop a few times anticipating if I should go back for my baby. I never like hearing him cry, my heart ached just by the thought. I kept going after encouraging myself it will all be over soon. This would be the last week for I can't do this!

With every step toward the bus stop was a step further away from my baby, and I couldn't get the scream of his cry out of my ear. I kept asking myself, are you making the right decision?

But again, I encourage myself with, I am going to get Shayne a present as I promise, to make up for making him go.

So now I was generated with excitement as to how happy they will be when they get back home to their gifts. The day went by and I got their gifts and was so excited to share it with them. I was all bubbly, just thinking about their reactions. That night, I went to my bed overly excited. Like a child, I couldn't wait for my babies to come home to their gifts.

It was Sunday morning, church as usual. Again it never felt the same, for my boys weren't home with me. Talking to God, as to how I am going to work things out. Monday was no school so Shermika and I had an agenda created for the boys.

I just couldn't wait!

Church was unusual this Sunday; the spirit of God was higher than ever. No service kept, just worship and prayers; it was beyond amazing. I remember asking God in the midst of the rich atmosphere, to cover my children, protect us from the unseen, and forgive me for all my sins known and unknown. I just felt like I needed to, so I did!

Church was over and my phone didn't ring, but I passed it off, as he must be having fun. It was unusual but it was a thought I could live with.

Went by Shermika as usual. As I entered the house, I went straight to the computer. I had promise my friend to help her with her assignment for school.

As I am using the computer, I saw an imagine pop up while communicating with my friend about the assignment. It rubbed me the wrong way, there was this dark cloud in the screen, and it gave me an unsettling feeling.

Looking at the time, I realize I didn't hear my babies' voices all day. Immediately, I looked for my phone to text Shayne.

Text: Shayne I love you, kiss Stephaune for me.

There was no respond, so I turn to Shermika showed her the picture and told her my thoughts.

She asked, "If I had spoken to him?"

I respond no, I text him but no answer.

She replied, "Call him."

I called him but there was no answer, I looked at the time and it was 6:35 p.m. I call again it went straight to voicemail, my thoughts now his battery is dead.

I then called my aunt and ask her to call their dad, she called back asking if I spoke to Steve (Shayne). I called him but got voicemail. She said she would try again, and call back. She called back saying, both phones going to voicemail.

I then told Shermika I was ready to go home. There was this new feeling of emptiness within. So I got my stuff together and we left.

She had to make a stop at the pharmacy before dropping me off. I was sharing with her my talk with God that morning. She listen and then turn to me and said, "your children are not your own, they were loan to you for a season."

"I know sis."

We kept talking till she dropped me off. When I thought she was home, I called. We said our good nights, after going over our itinerary for the next day. I spoke to another friend then my mom; we said our good nights and hung up.

There was this voice saying, rest you are going to need it. So I related it to my mom and told her good night, for I don't know why I need rest.

To bed I went but was awaken by a burning sensation in my back. It was though Stephaune was in my bed with me. I looked over and Shayne was lying peaceful in his bed. Shaking my head, opening and closing my eyes. I knew it couldn't be possible, for they both weren't home yet.

Still feeling Stephaune in my bed and seeing Shayne in his, I was now thinking, I must really miss my babies'.

Looking over at their gifts I whispered, "I must really miss you both, for now am seeing you both here."

I closed my eyes and decided I need to get that rest. So in my mind, I said a quick prayer and was off to sleep again.

# 9

# Moment of Truth

So my phone started ringing, but by the time I could answer it stopped. Looking at the time, it was after four a.m. Before I could think why my phone started ringing again. The calls kept coming in, but no one would answer me. When someone decided to say something, all they said was "hello" and they were off the phone. Then some would ask if others call me. At this time everything in me was saying, this is not good! Finally someone stayed on the phone, "Areka are my kids okay?"

"Why you went straight to the children?"

"I have gotten calls, one behind the other and no one wants to speak to me."

"Where you live?"

"Are my kids okay?"

"AJ drove left me to come to you."

"Are my children okay?"

"Is anyone with you?"

"Yes, but are my children okay?"

"AJ is on his way, when him come."

"Areka, is something wrong with my children?" She wanted to talk to who was there; I handed over the phone after knocking the door to wake someone up. They spoke then came to my room, to say they saying something's wrong. I told them I would get on Facebook, for if something happen it will be there. I had received an inbox message from their older sister that their dad was in the hospital. Immediately I logged off to call the operator. Got all the numbers for hospital in the counties. After calling a few, I found the girls in one hospital. The person I spoke to gave me two other numbers to call. I hung up and found their dad, got info on how he was doing, then the next number kept transferring me, from extension to extension.

Eventual I got to a man that wanted to know if I were alone and to speak with them. I handed over the phone then it was handed back to me. The words hit my ears like a tidal wave, "your sons have passed away."

I asked a few questions, for I needed to be sure. Eventually he humored me and answered my questions. I threw the phone on the bed, held my hands up, and started praying. Speaking directly to God, asking Him questions, I needed answers!

"Lord, how could this be, we spoke, I know it was you."

I needed to know three things?

How could my most loving child not hear I love you?

How could Stephaune not have a mother, when he needed it most?

How could this be, I need to know you were there?

"Shayne was my most loving child, so how could this be Lord, and Stephaune is too young to die alone, how could I not be there?"

As I looked around to walk out their room, there was AJ with his arms stretched out. In his arms I realize, this must be real.

Walking to my room, my thoughts, is it real though? Asking AJ repeatedly, he shook his head saying "yes."

"Does Laura mother know yet?"

"No"

"I got to go to her."

"Stacey you can't, you just lost the boys."

"I know, but I am a mother first, I got to go to her."

When we got there, AJ didn't want me to go; he thought I had enough on my plate. That's a day that still rest heavily on my heart, for I needed to do that, for only a mother that have lost would understand.

We came back to the house and all the arrangements started. The troopers came and left, then the owner of the funeral home. All this meant nothing to me, for it couldn't bring my babies' back.

Everyone started to come over, but I just really wanted my babies'. All I could reflect on is what we would have been doing at the hour or minute.

Condolences kept coming; I was busy with God for they said I couldn't see my boys, and would have to have a close casket ceremony. So I was busy looking for Him in the midst of it all.

My children faces were perfect, so how could it be? I couldn't see my babies' faces not one last time.

I was reminded of my statement as I lay in bed, "Say good-bye, for you won't see them again." Why? Why did I say that?

It's all part of the puzzle!

That evening, all I could think about was how could I create something to honor my boys?

Shermika cousin came to me and said to listen to the song 'Wrap Me in Your Arms.' So through the arrangements, that was included on everything.

MOTIVATED TO START THIS NEW VENTURE, FOR THIS WAS A WAY TO KEEP MY BOYS ALIVE.

I sat still unsettle, as to how God hasn't showed up? My three questions needed to be answered, so I could move on.

It was getting late and people were coming and going. Lost in my conversation with God. Shermika came to let me know her cousin was leaving. I told her she couldn't leave; she got something to tell me. She called her on the phone telling her to come back. I excuse myself and went outside to see her. I looked at her and said, "You have something to tell me." She respond unknowingly and before I could say God said, she started crying and doing her arms like Shayne did when he had the traveling pain.

It was strange, for I never told her of my experience. She kept saying, "I am okay mommy, I am okay." She continue going on and on asking me to look at her, I'm okay in a childlike manner. Asking, "Don't you see me, I'm alright." Tears streaming down her face, I stared at her, thinking God is good, how could this be?

Seeking my attention, she rests her head in my chest saying, "I'm okay now."

Interrupted by children stumbling over each other, laughing and playing. I stepped back, looking around, and wondering if anyone else was hearing it. When I couldn't stand it no more, for everyone eyes was on her, I distracted Shermika attention by asking her if she hear that.

She asks, "What?"

I responded, "Children playing."

She heard nothing, but I kept hearing giggles, so I had to ask, "You don't hear the giggles?"

"No sis that must be for you."

I kept listening, trying to figure it out.

"There is life after death" followed by more giggles.

"Did you hear that sis?"

She looked over at me with a questionable look.

The voice said "there is life after dead" and I made the giggling expression I heard.

She says, "It's Shayne."

"You hear it?"

"No, but that's so Shayne."

At that time I accepted it was just for me, and it was my angels confirming they are home with the Lord.

We then all talked for a while, then everyone left except Neisha. Her and me spoke for a while then got ready for bed.

Eventually I fell asleep but was soon to be woken by a feeling. When I got up, she was sitting up in the bed across from me. Her baby was asleep, but when I looked good, Shayne was behind her, I said nothing.

The morning we woke up, we sat talking. She said to me, that she was up because she never sense Shayne but sense Stephaune present.

I replied, "That's strange."

She responded surprise as to why I thought that to be strange, so I turned to her and said, "But when I woke and looked at you, Shayne was kneeling behind you looking at you."

Tears fill her eyes for she knew someone was there but she passed it off as something else.

The phone rang and the presence of God began to be a reality.

"Ms. Satchell, you can come and identify your boys."

At that very minute I was celebrating in my heart.

Hallelujah Jesus, hallelujah.

Immediately I grabbed my phone and called Shermika to come get me. Then rushed to bath and get ready to go, I popped my CD out the player, for I had it playing the whole night.

On our way, I couldn't but look at the weather it was so gloomy. I thought it reflected my emotions. My stomach was still full even though I never ate.

We got to the morgue and reality hit; it was true my babies' were gone forever. My mood was soon to change, for in the photos they showed of my babies were perfect. Their faces was intact, I never had to have a closed casket.

This meant the world to me, I had become the closest to my old self from I got the news. My perfect wasn't destroyed!

I shift in full gear, started functioning and thinking towards the preparations for the boy's funeral.

Still getting condolence calls and visits, going to bible study and doing my part as the intercessor at church.

Sitting in church and God is dealing with me about measuring my pain. I turned my book to a blank page and start to record what I was hearing.

God was taking care of me!

Two week went by and it was the wake, moment of truth, how will I feel? Unsure as to what to do, I braced myself and walked in. My world was once again turned upside down. They weren't perfect, could this be real. Lord, help me I whispered on the inside as tears stream down my face. Stephaune wasn't perfect, how could this be Lord? When I viewed their pictures, they looked nothing like this.

Torn between two loves, I stumbled over to Shayne casket. He looked more like himself but was damage.

Counting my time, I was back and forth.

Saying good-bye was very hard, for I couldn't hug and squeeze them, no kisses in return, nor I love you. They couldn't respond no matter how long I stood talking to them.

Growing up they say, children should bury their parent, but here I was burying two of my three birth children. Having another child was a thought by many, for I am young. But the fact is, they are irreplaceable, and secondly I can't have any more children.

Everyone else was being ushered in, so immediately I pulled myself together. My brother, Neisha, my cousins and all the children were breaking down. Someone had to give a shoulder for him or her to cry on. I went from holding up one person to another, rotating the best way I could.

My granddad kept holding my hand saying, "it's okay to cry, and we are here for you."

I kept giving him the same response each time, "I'm alright."

Then came the gentleman from the accident scene. He introduces himself and said he has a poem for the boys, gave condolence on behalf of his wife who couldn't make it for she was soon to have a baby, and then off to pay his respect. He excuses himself and went and paid his respect. It was personal, you could see love and hurt. It was remarkable, for this was a stranger but it felt like he knew them for a lifetime.

I was told that God said, I was to speak, baffled at the thought, I started talking to God. I went for my book that I had written in that Sunday in church, it was for tonight.

After reading about God measuring my pain, I freely began to speak. Then I went on to talking about my boys' life here on earth. I also played a part of Shayne favorite song by the Grits, 'My Life Be Like.'

When it was all over, my granddad walked up to me and said, "Why you didn't tell me, you were of God."

"I told you I was okay.'

I then went on to saying goodnight to others.

# 10

# The Funeral

It was time to say my final good-bye. The funeral morning was here and my thoughts are to not look again. So I braced myself as I walked through the church door. It was unavoidable; the caskets were at the entrance of the door.

I looked and saw the pain in their sisters' eyes and my heart wept for that was my child in pain and there is nothing I can do about it. At this moment I was so wishing Shaniece and Abigail could be there for she needed something that I believe only they could do for her…comfort.

Everyone knew of her love for her siblings but what she and Shayne had was different. I believe somehow they were made complete by each other. So with this knowledge I was like a broken vessel. I was lost as to the how to help her for there was no words to replace the hurt and pain she have inside.

I tried to comfort her asking if she wanted to come sit with me, but she wanted to just stare at the casket. My nurturing nature couldn't bring her peace for what she wanted most I wanted too, our Angels to come back to us.

In that minute as I walked away my heart was tearing apart for I couldn't help my child. So I begin to pray, asking the Lord to take my peace and give it to her for I can take care of me but she can't nor as I know won't let anyone in to help.

Trying to avoid seeing my boys I tried looking the other way as I walked slowly to my assigned seat. Still distracted by my daughter's pain, praying and hoping all be well with her and that being around the other child from the accident she may be open to talking about her feelings and that all the right answers be given for I need that more than anything.

At my seat now, talking to God as to how I am going manage here after for there is no turning back. This is it my final good byes. It was the strangest mix of emotions, for though I was missing them beyond imagination; I was at peace.

As everyone settled down all I could think about was how is she doing? So I kept looking around the church to see where she was and what she was doing. Finally I found peace within when I saw her in the arms of Areka. I was happy for I know she would feel the love and find some comfort in she is not alone.

The service started and as always the Lord was there in the midst of it all, I could feel His presence. Everyone had such wonderful things to say about my boys; though I wish the occasion were different I was thankful in all things for my children.

It was a battle over the weeks of preparation, if I was capable and ready to read at the service. Though everyone else had his or her opinions, which I was thankful and respectful of, I was confident I could for God favors me. So I was able and did the reading of my boys' obituaries' and a tribute to them both. I must say everything went well even with the little glitch here and there. They had a wonderful celebration and sending home service. The minister delivered and souls were set free from the word that was fed to us. Lives changed that day and for that I am eternally grateful to the man of God for allowing God to use him.

The service was over and it was time to get ready to go to the cemetery as I look around at all the support I was receiving I was overwhelm with excitement for I had my family, friends, student and their parent, teacher and principal, even friends that travel from across the states and my home country just to be here for me in my time of bereavement. In this moment I was thankful for God was showing up all through my experience as I requested that morning I received the tragic and terrifying news.

As everyone came over to say hi and give their condolences my eyes was on my daughter, still wondering what is going to happen to her?

Praying that I will one day have the opportunity to help her go through this horrid experience in her life.

As a mother the worst feeling is, you not being able to help your child/ren when they need you the most. As always my heart was being torn between my loves'. I was at the service, at the hospital and in Jamaica all at the same time. It was all I could do think about my three princesses. Thankful that she made it to service for I believe she needed closure. At the hospital in my mind wondering if I think about her long enough she would feel my presence and know that mommy is there with her every step of the way as she recover from her surgeries. Celebrating in my heart that I have so many love ones back home that loves us so much, which gave me peace that Shan is well taken care of, even though more than anything else I just want to hug my princess and tell her the news and reassuring my baby that all will be okay.

I played around in my mind of what the day will be like when Abbi and Shan learn that their brothers have passed away. Praying that I be the one to tell them both for it wouldn't be good if I didn't do it for only their mother can bring comfort in their time of pain.

Everything was passing me by as I stood in a gaze as to what is going to happen now that it is done. My boys are gone and my girls are separated in the time when they need each other the most. Control was ripped away from my hands and there was nothing I could do but pray.

My attention was refocus by the hugs of love ones still offering their condolences. Then by the chauffeur instructing me to be seated as she closed the door of the limo so the procession could begin.

Speaking to my grandparent and friend in the car as I gazed through the window at the facial expressing of people as we pass them by. Still in my own little world as to how am I going to bring peace to my girls?

How are they going to manage day to day?

How could I turn back the hands of time?

I know all this wasn't possible and that I had to rely on God to do all this for them, and me but my heart couldn't rest knowing my daughter was in pain and the two younger one will someday soon have to learn the reality of the death of their brothers.

Needing a pickup now more than ever I excuse myself from the conversation and turned my attention to the Lord for I need to be refuel. Staring into nowhere I ask God, seeing that things are going to slow down now, am I still going to be able to go on like I have with all the distractions of planning the funeral and going to the hospital and taking care of my family?

The ratio has change, for the only thing to do now is take care of my love ones as they heal from this experience.

The car is slowing down as we pull off the road into the cemetery; reality rears its ugly head again. It's time to say my final good bye.

Pulling up to the burial spot I see a tent and chairs to the side. Taking a deep breath in as the driver came out to open my door. Looking around as am escorted to my assign seat by the grave. All I could feel was pain as I walked up to my seat, which was soon replaced by emptiness.

Listening to all the sobbing with my head held down wondering what is this now Lord?

As the words are being said over the grave, a voice said within look up. I slowly lift my head wondering what was to come.

It was she I was well please. Is she supposed to be here? I don't know but I was pleased.

Staring at her hoping she doesn't see me, still wondering if she should be. God seem to always be a step ahead of me. So much peace fell upon me for the love and never ending support I was receiving was amazing.

It's a wonderful thing to see the beauty of love through someone eyes. For though CeCe didn't know me, she showed up at my boys' graveside it mean the world to me and gave me the courage and strength to keep going.

Praising God within as to how wonderful He is. Why she stood there as part of my family I knew not at this time but was grateful. As I always say God is a step ahead of us always sometimes more.

She was supposed to be just a lady doing her job, filling out paper work for customers as they come to purchase lots for their love ones but she have been a source of healing in my time of pain.

Never will I forget the way I felt when I lift my head and she was standing there. Even now as I type these words I am still celebrating what she has done for me. God placed her in my life to help with my healing process and I am grateful for she listened to what the Lord gave her instruction to do.

Looking around at everyone by the graveside as my boys are being lowered in the ground, a feeling of worry is in their eyes for me. Thankful but at the same time hoping they see that God is taking care of me.

Feeling a sharp pain within I paid attention to the where it was coming from. Looking out at the direction I feel it coming from and there my brother stooped at the graveside looking in. My thoughts are, my poor baby get up.

Knowing that it wasn't going to happen I stood to my feet with my hand towards him praying that he leaves room for the Lord to come in and heal his broken heart.

Once again I felt that emptiness and it was coming from in the ground, so looking down thinking to myself, its empty my Angels aren't here.

Then beside me was Brent doing the same thing, looking in. He then walked away without a word said. For the first time I wasn't worried about him, he was going to be okay a voice whispered to me. Not given much thought to the why because it always reveals itself.

So it was over and everyone was talking and making arrangement to head back to the church for that's where the repast was taking place.

Back in the car and being driven back to the church for the repast. Now in the church hall fellowshipping with each other it was visible to me what some were thinking and feeling towards me throughout this process of losing my sons.

Some were in fear of me falling out one day for the need to break was necessary for me to heal but what they didn't know was that I was 'Beautifully Broken'. While others were amazed at what God was doing in me for it was visible to them and they too became hungry for what they saw within me. One conversation so present in my mind is of my uncle's wife. As she expressed her thoughts of how impossible it was to reach me to extend her condolences for either I was at church or out making sure all arrangements met my needs. It was obvious she need God in the way she never knew He existed.

Words can't express how grateful and thankful my heart was throughout this process though my loss was great and unimaginable, God showed up throughout every area of this experience in my life. He was taking care of my debts, catering to all my needs, comforting me at the same time; the never-ending blessing of the Lord was in everything done. Before I knew it, it was done!

When I first got the news lost was the way to describe me but as reality set in it was obvious to me that so much were needed to be done. I remember praying and asking the Lord how could this be for I don't know how I am going to afford this funeral and how could He allow me to give my last in church knowing it would be need?

As I prepared for bed one night, I remember praying on end as to how all this is going to be possible and those are the very question I asked of the Lord. He answered me and said, "Out of your obedience watch me work."

Blasted away by this, anxiety consume me for my need to share was burning my lips. As soon as the sun could rise over the east I was up and in excitement to tell Shermika of what had happen. She replied, "Well watch and see."

It is obvious God showed up and showed out in every area needed and some. God made a way for me out of nowhere.

It is God that girdeth me with strength and maketh my way perfect. Psalms 18:24 (KJV)

# 11

# Life after the Fact

So the funeral was over and people where getting back to their perspective lives. Arrangements were being made and I was going to spend time with family and friends for everyone thought it to be in my best interest at the time. For months I visited family, some I haven't seen in a long time and others that I been in communication with over the years. It was a time well needed but in the midst of it all, the only thing I wanted to do was curl up in a room with no one to bother me. That has not happened yet, not even now. Busy seem to be my new lifestyle no time for a pity party.

My days were spent, praying, reading the Word and traveling to conferences. As the days and weeks went by I was growing spiritually which made the world harder to live in. Wishing everyday if only I could find a place alone to escape from all the thoughts am hearing. If we were sharing the same space your thoughts were mine, and it hurt for they were all about me.

Why was everyone expecting for me to fall out?

Am I supposed to fall out?

Am I doing something unusual?

Praying to the Lord asking Him to please show me how to cry for I can't seem to do what everyone is expecting of me.

Why Lord, why am I not cry?

Am I wicked?

Am I heartless?

What is it Lord?

What is it?

No answers yet, as I paced the floor wishing I could have one last hug, one last kiss, one last 'I love you mommy'. Staring at their picture upon the wall, trying to feel what others are expecting of me. Today I asked myself why I did that but through my experience it was thought to me, it was a part of the process, Gods divine plan for my life.

Lost in a place of acceptance, I need to know the what to do so that others will realize that I am not a selfless person but I feel and hurt it's just that I may do it in a different way. Why? For God designed me this way for His purpose.

So I went to my bed that night caught up on the how I was going to help others understand my process. Missing my boys like crazy wasn't making it any better for me to see the bigger picture and design.

Laying in the sofa sleeping and Shayne came up to me and said that I should awake and come with him. Following his lead I went where he lead me, he said mommy you can't stay long I am going to take you to see Stephaune.

Where is he?

He responded just come mommy just come.

In this place I was able to hug and kiss my Angels and tell them how much I love and miss them. Its unexplainable but it was as though I was in a different realm. Enjoying every moment of it for it was so real as though they never died but in the very instant I knew they were but it was just so real. Interrupted by Shayne's' voice mommy you have to go, come and he lead me back to my rest and I was awoken as he hugged me so tightly.

Jumping up out my sleep looking around the living area wondering what was that. Feeling on myself for it felt as though is arms where still wrapped around my arms. Tears fill my eyes once again flattered by the awesome work of God for yet again He perceived my imagination. For never would I ever imagine something like this could ever happen. Sitting upright I pondered at that what had happened and praising God at the same time for though I can't explain what has happen I was happy beyond measure.

Thinking to myself will anyone ever believe me that this just happen?

How was it possible?

Seeing I couldn't explain to myself I was mindful as to whether or not someone would believe it happened. Mesmerize by my experience and celebrating at the same time for now I'm thinking God has my back. I am special my thoughts to myself I'm not alone for God is truly with me. Excited to share with the sis Shermika for she I know will understand that it was Gods doing.

She was excited for me as always, in all I do she is always there for me, no matter who she has to stand up to she got my best interest at heart.

Still at a lost as to why the ones around me still fear for me believing I am heartless I was torn inside. Happy for my experience but needed to know, why am I not crying?

So about a week went by and I was looking for answers as to why I'm not crying?

Why am I so courageous after all I have lost?

As always God never leave me hanging, He showed up! He took me back to the week before my boys passing and I asked Him why am I here?

No respond but as I looked around I realize I was reliving that Sunday in church when I couldn't pray. Watching as it all played out, it was then I realize why I was there. As I once again laid on the ground and wept a voice emerge and said' "You did cry, I allowed you to then for I am going to need you."

I was ecstatic and excited all in one. When I woke up my first reaction was to call Shermika and tell her to remind me to tell her what had happen when she see me again.

Another month had pass and I was making arrangement to be a part of the celebration that was to occur in August 2011 for they were honoring the earth Angels that played a part in the helping out on the scene of the accident.

This was perfect timing for I need to meet these people for I had only spoken to them over the phone or through Facebook, and this was also my time to share with my sis my most recent super natural experience.

So the planning starts for I had to be there for this celebration. In everything I did it wasn't possible. Again God was ahead making my way clear. Every plan fell through and I was unable to make it up to Ft. Pierce where the event was held. By the evening, speaking to Joy it was obvious that God redirected my path. It would have been ugly she said, she was happy I didn't make it. She is still being an angelic presence in my life. Though she not jumping in excitement for the recognition I'm still thankful for her and she is and will forever be one of my earth angels.

So my princess had still not known that her brothers had pass even though she had been back home in American for one month now. Moment of truth wasn't too far away for, she been asking for them every day since she got back home. So we went to the cemetery to look for the boys. Before I could musk up the courage to say anything she popped out the question, "Mommy can you read what's on those stick please?"

Looking at her knowing at that very moment she had identified their names for it was one of the things we did in our playtime, learning to spell each other's name.

"It says Shayne and Stephuane"

She looked at me as she started to cry and said, "Mommy you lying"

My heart fell to the ground but no time to waste I quickly pulled myself together.

Running towards her I held her by her hands and stoop to the ground, "Look at me honey" She tried not to but I continued, "Do you believe mommy would lie to you"

At that moment she stopped pulling her hand away from me and looked me in my eyes and then walked back to the grave.

Staring at her my heart is broken into pieces for now I have the job of helping her heal. It was expected to not be easy but God has the last say. We spent some time by the graveside in mostly silent and then we were off to spend the rest of day with Amarii and Neisha that was there with us.

Throughout the day I wasn't present at all for the only thing on my mind was when the alone time comes for the questions are sure to follow. So inside prayer was all I could do so I prayed.

We went home and thanks to God she was too tired she fell asleep. It was pleasure to this mom's heart for it was a lot to deal with.

Finally I got the time to be alone with Shermika, for she needed to hear of my most recent experience and all that has happened over the pass few months, we had to play catch up and it was perfect for Shan needed them as they all needed her. We were all sharing in the experience of losing our boys for they were her son's brothers and it was sad to know our family has suffered a shift such as this one.

As I shared with her what had happen she was enlighten by it all for she remembers the day all too well? It was she who had laid her hand in my back that day and it was her curiosity as to what had happen at the altar.

Bringing back to her remembrance as to what it was she had asked me and what my respond was. She looked at me as her memories came flooding back. Allowing her to see God amazing work for herself, I then looked at her and said exactly as the voice said to me that day I first relieved it. She was excited and she too started to realize that, my prosperity was in the arms of the Lord, and that I'm okay.

Thinking I need to get my life on the right path now for my baby girl need some stability after all that she has been through.

The deception started, everyone I thought I could trust I couldn't. Being blood related meant nothing. Back to my way of thinking my family is those that God has given me, as hard as I have prayed for a place to belong it was high time I start being appreciative of those the Lord as given me. From sisters to father to mamma and poppa, nephews and a wonderful extended family that just love me for who I am and not for what I can do for them or the who they wish me to be.

Being alone was a thing of the pass, my family was beautiful and they are mine to love and appreciate all the days of my life.

# 12

# Part of the Healing Process

As I seek for more directions as to where to go and what to do for it was evident that something had to happen or the cycle would replay itself again. The truth is I'm grateful for all God has done for me but was sure I couldn't do it again, so I was back to making sure my daughter and I were protected for the fight wasn't over just yet.

Creating a plan as to what to do to keep us protected. I conjured up a plan of survival for I couldn't bury another child, I just couldn't, so I ran with ever strength in me with my daughter by my side. Shan's safety was my responsibility and seeing that she still had life for my decision paid off when I packed her up and send her to be with my older brother and family back home. So I did the only thing I know to do protect my daughter with all my might and wit.

Feasting on all I had been through and all the magical experiences I was bless to be a part of, in that very moment it was apparent to me that this too I will overcome. My daily life was encourage by everyone that played a part in my healing process but it wasn't over yet there was room to grow and battles to concur. Only difference this time I was prepared and had reinforcement like never before. As I go along you will see how your greatest encouragements will come from the place you least expect it and the power in which it inhabits will take you through your pain and into your restoration.

As always my way of growing is through reading, so I went searching for a book I had gotten from Shayne's second grade teacher from the first time he attended Atlantic West Elementary in 2008.

'From Pain to Promise' was the name of the book it was written by herself and her husband. They too had lost a child and for this said reason I believe she thought it would bring me peace. As I read the book it brought me back to a place where comfort and peace was given unto me from the precious children from Shayne Schools. It kept me grounded and in great peace for the words of these amazing children was right on point it was just what I needed then and even in this moment as I'm reflecting on the words while reading this book, my comfort and peace level peeked.

Again it is proven that even out of babes we find strength and praise. Being sensitive to the spirit you will find help in all places, even in the deepest darkest place you can find encouragement.

Psalms 8:2 (NIV)

You have taught children and infants to tell of your strength, silencing your enemies and all who oppose you.

I'M ALWAYS LOOKING FOR THE GOOD IN MY BAD SITUATIONS

## Letter from Ramblewood Elementary School Principal

Steve Shayne Hansen was a fourth grader at Ramblewood Elementary and had only recently withdrawn and returned to Atlantic West Elementary. I first became acquainted with Shayne when he was a second grader and need to get home from school on a hot September afternoon. Mom had just had baby and both Shayne and Abigail needed to get home. They had been accustomed to walking but we managed to find someone to drive them home and Shayne was very appreciative and made sure his younger sister was always safe. I remember Shayne as a quiet, petit young man with beautiful eyes that were always watching and observing everything around him.

Once we heard the tragic news about the accident, a Crisis Team called to both Ramblewood Elementary and Atlantic West to assist student and adults in dealing with the event. When I asked students to describe Shayne and tell me what he was like as a classmate, one student said, "Shayne was just cool". When asked to tell what that meant, he explained, Shayne was helpful to others and very funny. He cared about his friends and classmates, Shayne was very thoughtful, he liked to skateboard and was very athletic, he was always happy and he told funny jokes. Shayne had become friends with a classmate in another room and they both lived at Sherwood Forest apartments. When he learned the terrible news, the child burst into tears and said that Shayne had protected him from the other kids at the apartment and he would miss him very much. He went on to simply say that Shayne was always joyful. Wow, an unusual word coming from a fourth grader to describe his friend. In addition, many of them said they would always remember Shayne and keep him in their hearts. Coming from someone who was working with children for many years, I know that when something tragic like this happens, students never forget and as a result, they will always carry a memory of Shayne with them forever.

Not only did students write memories about Shayne, but they also wrote comments to Shayne's mom and family, since they knew how sad you must be. They wanted you to know that you had a one of a kind son that he is in a special place and he will always watch over you.

Another offered a tip that helped her deal with something tragic like this and that was to always stay busy during difficult times and they sincerely hope that joy will come again to you and that you feel better soon.

Steve Shayne Hansen will always be in the hearts of those who knew him. Shayne made an impression on those he came in contact with and will be missed by all.

"Do you hear what these children are saying?"

"From the lips of children and infants you Lord have called forth your praises'." (Partial quotes From the NIV Matthews 21:16)

I haven't known your son for very long, He was a very good person f the short amount of time that I knew him. I have been to alot of different schools, and i my whole childhood I have never heard that word (killed) in a sentence with other classmate's name. I wished I would never have to experience that but in Coral springs Florida 2001 I did experience it. My classmate has passed. He will be remembered by alot of ~~one~~ in the school of Ramblewood Elementary. I remember him and I barely knew him. He will not be missed just from kids in his school, but from teachers, freinds, and family. I hope no one will have to take in what some of the people in Ramblewood Elementary took in. The family of Shane, You guys are very lucky to have such a bright and wonderful son. I think you should know that you have such a ~~~~ of a kind son. You should remember your son as kind, generous, smart, and there is to much more to say about him. If you were here right now (parents) You should see how people care about your son. You should be very very proud of your son and how many friends he has made.

I wrish you guys the best of luck.
From Jake Washecka Friend and classmate.

April 5, 2011 Coral springs Florida Ramblewood Elementary.

Dear Mrs. Hanson,

We all feel teribly sorry and sad. We all Loved him very much. But as his mother, I know how you feel and we want to help you through this.

Love,
Chloe

Dear, Shanes mom      April 5, 2011

Shane was a great kid. He was like my best friend. When He moved to a different class I was kind of sad. He was kind of quiet but he was friendly. Sometime he will share with other people. But shanes mom don't be sad because he's in a special place and he will watch over you. Shane will always be in your heart we all loved Shane. You also created a very nice and ittellegent boy. I miss him too

           Sincerly
           Brayden

we love Shane

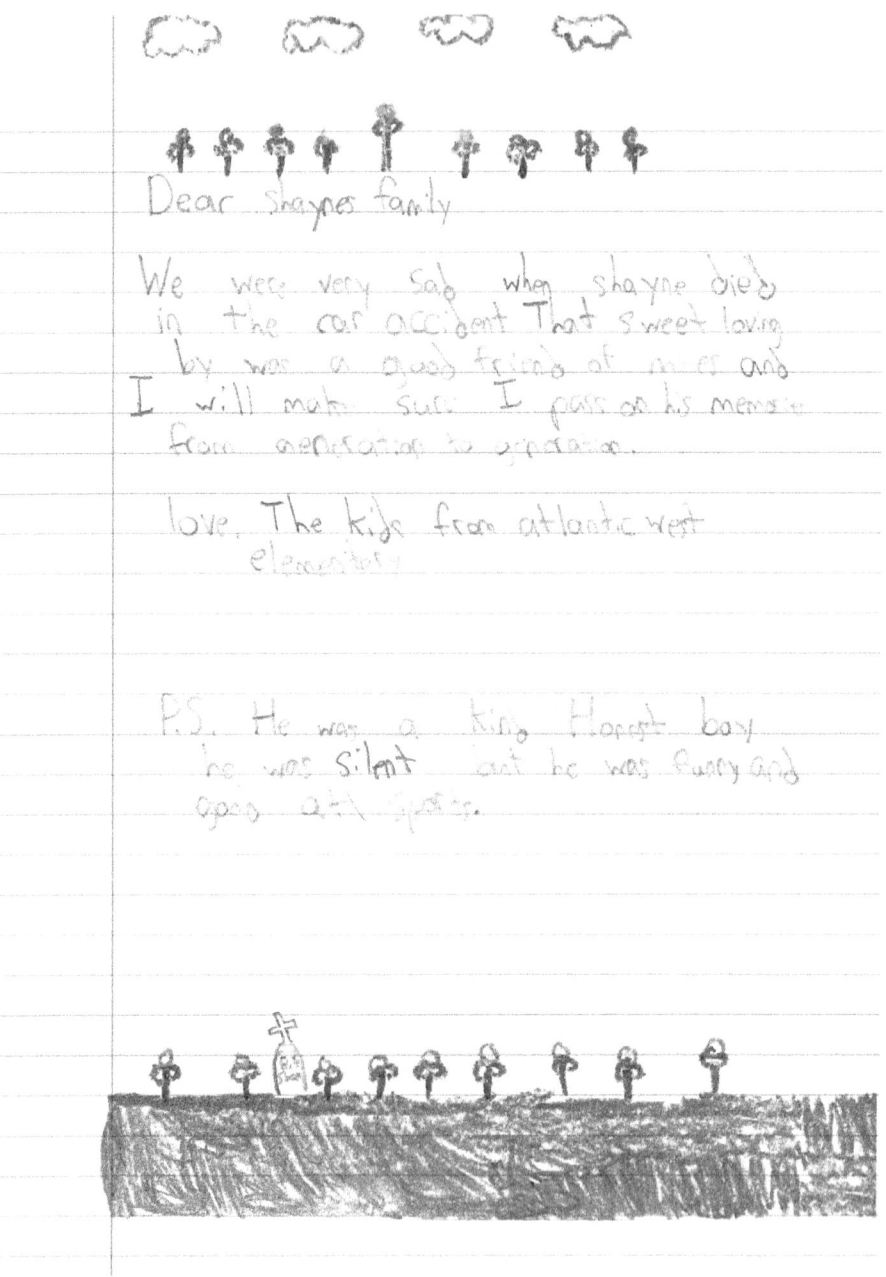

Dear Shaynes family

We were very sad when Shayne died in the car accident. That sweet loving boy was a good friend of mines and I will make sure I pass on his memory from generation to generation.

love, The kids from atlantic west elementary

P.S. He was a kind, Honest boy he was silent but he was funny and good at sports.

Mike Joseph
4-5-11

Dear Hansen family,

Our entire classroom heard about the tragic loss of your son Shayne he was a very Athletic child. Me, Stevens, and Brian had the same Intrest in WWE wrestling. At P.e. he really knew how to get people out in dodgeball. He got me out of the game about 4 times. He was very smart and quiet but outside he had a good sense of humor. For the one day I knew him I knew we be best friends. Our class wishes you and your family the best of luck and we will miss him very much! We all will see him in Heaven!

In loving memory of Shayne hansen,

Mike Joseph

Dera shayne hansen family

I so srroy wot happen to your son shayne wen I frist saw your son I saw that he will be his beat friend he is so so good at dodgeball I was in his time and I now us won the game and no one could not take him out ever time someone threw he now was they was throwing it was like he read there mide everone was shoke how neone could take him out he was the nice friend in the how werld

from Shayne beat friend stevens

P.S. I am so srroy wot happen to your son

Dear Shanes parents

My name is Kystaleigh Shane was my best friend he sat by me at school and I can tell you a lot about him. His favorite color is blue, green, white, black. Loves WWE rasaling. He's from Jamaica. He loves to be called by Shane not Steve and he as great in PE and dageball we were best friends and we even had plans for 5th grade. Well I wish you luck and may Shane rest in peace

P.S I'll never forget him he will always be my bff ♡

Love, Krystaleign

P.P.S. he wanted to open a WWE company so now he can

♡ Good Luck Shane

Dear Shayne's family
   I am so sorry what happen to your son Shayne he was a good friend of mine. He was really good at dodgeball and he was sporty and fun to play and talk to he was really funny I miss him so much, he was so quiet he did his work I miss him so much I want him back to play with and have him back in our class so you guys could have him as a family to.

   sincerly shayne's friend
   Symon

Dear Shayne's family,
Shayne was the best friend a boy could ever have he had a great sense of humor the best dodgeball player in the class he was one of my best friends in the entire school, I miss him like he was a family member of mine. The second he stepped in the room I knew we would be great friends.

Really Sad boy: Scott Phan

To: Shayne's family

From: Chandler Sackram

Dear, Shayne Hancock family

I am so sorry for what happend about Shayne during that car accident on the road. As a cool friend when saw him in class when we were in Second grade we had shared lots of friendship. And now I saw him again in fourth grade he had a good sense of humor and he loved to play his most favoritist game dodgeball.

Sencerily, Chandler Sackram

ps. I am so sorry for that awesome friend.

Dear, Shayne's family,

I've heard about Shayne died in the car accident We all loved Shayne and I'm going to miss him a lot. We loved how he played dodgeBall. I was his friend at sharewood forest too. We always play BasketBall and catch or real footBall. we sometimes play our BeyBlade outside he was like a Best friend and I'll never forget aBout Shayne and our fun times togeter we all wish he was here right now

Sincerely,
Brian

I have seen life being birth in me, and hope being deposited through these children. One, which will last me a lifetime for it was a part of my healing process, which helped deliver me from my reality nightmare, which will forever be apart of my testimony.

In my heart I carry these precious little angels for I love and appreciate them with all my heart, they have encourage my spirit life and given me purpose to keep pressing forward for they have thought me that victory is mine and I receive it and carry it as a torch in dark places.

At this time in my life thanksgiving is all I could do for I kept seeing the marvelous work of God in my life throughout every situation of my life. He was present on the scene of the accident and he was present in every situation from the planning of the funeral to refilling me on my off days and moments to the blocks and hurdles He created to keep me safe.

In every area He showed up and laid is hand on and in, for situations where being transform from pain to restoration. Three question had I asked that first day when the news hit, my ear.

"How could this be, I need to know you were there?"

"How could Stephaune, not have a mother, when he needed one most?"

"How could my most loving child not hear 'I love you'?"

 The first two where answered but seeing that it was said that the boys died before impact was finish, I told myself to settle for at least you got two of the three Stacey. Still trusting God with what I had receive for the truth is I found peace that day just knowing they felt no pain nor did they have to miss or worry for me.

GOD MEASURED MY PAIN

# 13

# The Truth Revealed

So now I'm confident that I can do all things but as always something as to cause you to shake. Doing my part in dotting all the 'i's and crossing all the 't's and then reality hits like a ton of bricks.

How am I going to live without being able to visit my boys as I choose?

I miss them so much and with Shan missing them so much it's hard.

How do I take her pain away?

How?

The flesh is having a pity party of its own.

Thinking about packing up my life and never looking back my heart is being separated into small bits and pieces. As I lay in the sofa that song keeps playing in my head, 'Precious Child.' I kept listening to the words as they played in my head and there was this one part that kept repeating and I know that's what Shayne wanted me to remember.

It said, "In my dreams you are alive and well, in my mind I see you clear as a bell, in my soul there is a hole that can never be filled. But in my heart there is hope for you are with me still, in my heart you live on always there never gone. Precious child you left too soon, though it may be true that we are apart, you will live forever in my heart.

Smiling at this for Shayne was that child who knew beforehand that I will be okay and that this too would I overcome.

As I hum the words I fell asleep repeating, "Precious child you both have left me too soon, though it may be true that we are apart, forever in my heart you both will live, forever in my heart."

Awoken by a hand I looked up and went, I was in a place that looked like a pasture the grass was so green and luscious it felt so surreal. I kept glancing over but couldn't see who was leading me so looking at the grass and my surrounding trying to figure out where am I?

It took about a second for me to realize where it was; I was at the cemetery where my boys were laid to rest. It was then I spoke, "Why am I here?"

A voice replied, "I have taken you this far and I will take you the rest of the way."

It was strange and rewarding at the same time, my feet felt like they never touched ground but those words will live in me forever. The words from that song comes to mind, 'Lord You're Might,' the words 'No words to express how great you are,' are so real to me in this moment. Its true we serve a mighty God!

Quick to wake and without any though praising the Lord is all I could do, thankful isn't even enough to express my gratitude to the Lord for He has truly taken care of me. Being on top of the world is all I felt. Who could touch me? No one!

So I got a message on Facebook from Jeanne and I was excited to meet up with her. Sending her my address and phone number to get in touch so we could go for a quick bite and talk about the accident.

The morning she came to get me excitement and anxiety set in. In my mind pondering what was to come but was sure that The Lord will give

what was needed to deal with it for my confidence level was up from my latest spiritual encounter.

We went to a quaint little diner it was nice and always refreshing to just get out the house. For other than church it had to be necessary and of great importance for me to go outside.

We had breakfast and talk about what my experience been like and she then started to share what had happen at the scene of the accident. I was astounded my mind explode, it was like a rocket launching from earth to space.

When I say God was measuring my pain believe me it truly is, He was sure to create a written expression of what He was doing for me from the beginning of this journey. Those words I wrote in church where still being proven day to day for here it is that God is yet again measuring my pain once again.

The words rolled off her lips in slow motion, "Shayne was still alive when I went over to him." What did she just say?

Shock is an understatement as to what I was feeling in that moment. Wanting to cry but my tears where held back by a voice in my head saying isn't this what you wanted, you don't have to settle anymore for all three questions have been answered.

It was in that instant the tears stream down my face, tears of joy. Mix emotions trying to pierce its way through my mind. My baby must have been in so much pain, worrying what is mommy going to do now?

The conversation went on and I was reassured that he wasn't in pain. All the medical terms were given but the only thing that made sense was he wasn't in any pain. It was obvious that she too realizes that I was missing from the scene and must be wishing it were different so she comforted him with kind words.

It soothes the pain that was raging through my chest like wild fire. My tears where now burning my eyes for they were constant for I just really wish this all didn't happen.

Sharing with her how loving he was and how not being able to be there for Stephaune was a torment but in the same minute a test of Gods great work was now my reality and coming testimony. He was doing a new thing in me and in this time we live in. Honored I am but missing them will never change for this is a wound that time cant heal but God can restore and give me peace as I go through it.

She then told me of how she felt the need to tell Shayne she love him. The room lit up like lights in a dark stadium, the words I needed to hear most, were no longer a wish but a true reality. She spoke to my baby and gave him great comfort in his passing and most important he heard the words "I love you."

Sweet music to my ears, my baby was at peace in his last moment and all the dots where connected, God truly showed up and continually takes care of me. His will was on course and I was following His lead. She also told me about the lady name Pam who was with my baby Stephaune being his mother for the night. At this moment I was well please thinking there truly nothing else one could desire after this. We finished up our meal and continued talking on our way to drop me off.

Putting this all out here is huge for even as I type and put this book together my family still don't know Shayne didn't die before the impact was over but lived a while before passing.

How do I pluck up the courage to do so?

Truth is I don't know.

However I will have to eventually do so for I can't publish this book and have them read of it when I have known all these months and not tell them. Feeling the need to protect them all from this for they are not spiritually grown enough yet to come to acceptance like I have for I wanted more than anything else that day the news of their death was given that my precious children were taken care of even in death.

Back home I bask in the glory of my Lord, more great works to add to my long list of great works He has done in my life. Anxious to now publish this book but the timing wasn't right, there was more room to grow.

A few months had pass and I tried to finish this book. Talking to a dear friend of mine, Sherie encourage me that there was more story to write, "it wasn't finish yet'" she said.

Taking her word for it and made a conscious decision to take this well need brake from writing this book. For it acquiesce with my spirit that it was true and I was entering in a new battle at this very moment. Praying about it like I did everything else and then off to my bed after reassuring myself that I have a track record that speaks for itself.

AWAITING MY NEW CHALLENGE

# 14

# Almost Complete

So I set the books aside, all four of them thinking that when the right time to continue comes it will be obvious and the books or book be completed. Life went on as usual, more trials and tribulations came. It didn't affect me for I was growing more with each day.

Something was missing but I didn't quite know what it was but was pretty sure that it will reveal itself. Being frustrated on some days, and smiling on others, for things weren't happening, as I would hope them to. Not always were the results as I wanted them to be but making well with whatever it was is the way I dealt with those obstacles.

To share with you some of my more awesome days, which always include me counseling someone and realizing it was first for me, or my daughter doing something miraculous.

Shaniece would do the things that aren't the norm and if you never see it, it's hard to believe that it happened but I guess she is my reward from God, my precious gem. There were so many days that she would relate to me what Shayne or Stephaune says or what God says, giving me directions or just simply comforting me.

This day in particular I was in the sofa about to just cry for I was missing my boys deeply and didn't know what else to do but cry for talking to them and getting no answers was painful. She burst through the room door and wrapped her arms around my neck tight as she utter, "Shayne says you are going to be okay mom."

Looking at her thinking how could she have known I was at a breaking point when she was in the other room watching television. Nothing can explain what had happen so I just leave it as, a higher power.

She would deliver messages saying Stephaune says he love you mommy or he says it isn't your fault mommy. Still mesmerize as to what happen and why all these unlikely things were happening to me. She sure is shining as a gem, what more could I ask for?

Even with all this I was still missing something, what?

Wasn't quite sure but it was obvious to me, something was missing. Being distracted by day-to-day events from reliving the boys' accident for case purposes to dealing with people without a heart or conscience, I was becoming a bit disconnected and I felt it.

Searching my mind as to what to do to fill this void, I turned to jogging in the mornings. It was there that my one and one time with God was rebuilding.

Talking to God each morning as to what to do and the when to do? Every day was pretty much the same but I needed more. Happy with what I had but knew I needed something else. What? Still not sure yet!

They're days when the tide got so high I don't see how I'm going to tread through it. One day in particular my frustration was through the roof and I needed to vent so calling my dad was always the thing that soothes me the most. He got the touch and right words to calm his daughter down. As I'm about to start the venting a voice said minister to him, no thought I started to minister into his spirit. A selfless act freed me from the torment within and helped him, which makes me happy for my belief is that one should honor their parents. The word as always has been for me first so in other words I helped me by helping him.

Every time I would minister into someone spirit my own situation always gets heal for before you can help someone with any issue you have to be set free from it yourself.

These where just a few of my trials for there was so much healing to be done in me for there was so much going on inside than I knew of but as they were uprooted my testimony get longer. Which means I am able to help more people.

With that said, on to my next issue that needed to be uprooted. As always something as to happen before you sometimes realize you have hidden issues.

Some time had passed and home as usual my phone rang and my dad asked the question, "how is our baby?"

Hmmm

I didn't really have an answer for I was blank as to what he was talking about.

"How is Abigail?"

"The last I heard of her she was okay."

He gestured that we need her home for just assuming and wondering wasn't enough. In that moment I wasn't really interested for the torment hadn't stopped but thanks to my lawyer Leslie who did everything in her power to make the pain minimal for me.

She understood that my healing process was nearly impossible for there was always something else, so she did her best to minimize what and how much I know. It had to be necessary or of great importance for her to get me involve. I thank God for her each and every day for she did a tremendous job looking out for my well being and trying to help me heal.

So jogging in the morning and talking to God as usual, when I got to the end of my thirty plus blocks, I begin to worship God it was the norm but I was up for a new experience.

Found myself crying and praying and singing at the same time. Soon the only thing I was able to do was cry. Weeping at the pain of not having my two daughters with me, bent over the railing on the boardwalk wanting to stop and just couldn't stop. God was dealing with another issue that was bottled up in that place I kept secret for years. That place where I could hide everything knowing no one could see what was in it or could they get to it but with God that is never the case.

Soon I was able to utter some words, all mumbled up, "I want them Lord,"

"Why are you allowing me to feel this?"

"I really don't want to deal with this Lord!"

Looking up into the sky I start praying and asking the Lord to set me free from this pain that's trapped inside of me. I needed to be, for I couldn't take it anymore. It was becoming unbearable!

Out of nowhere I felt it. Four set of hands wrapped around me. One by my bust line, one by my waistline, one on my shoulders and one by my face. It was my girls and my boys they all were with me that very moment. Peace fell upon me and the pain just seems to slowly seep out.

I worshipped the Lord so hard, giving Him thanks for allowing me to have this supernatural experience, and in that moment I accepted that things would someday be as I hope it to be.

Jogging back home, all smiles across my face. Butterfly flutters in my heart, gratitude written in my eyes.

Time had pass by and for the first I could rest assure that my prayers where reaching my daughters. The day Shan had told me that Shayne and God had gone to be with the girls was my confirmation that they are protected.

Being the perfectionist that I am complete satisfaction was never mine for I am always hoping they know in their hearts they haven't been forsaken. Something else I have to work on is to just let go and let God.

There where those days when I had to be the rock for my little princess Shaniece, for she has been that for me so many times before. She would have her off days when she just miss her brothers and wanting them back.

She would ask questions such as, "Mommy can God just do this one thing for us and bring my brothers back to life."

"Why did they have to die mommy?"

"Will we ever see them again?"

"I know they are dead mommy, but why my brothers?"

Listening to my baby girl as she goes on and on with these questions, my heart is being severely damage. Wanting with all my might to give her back her brothers, even though I know I can't. Shaking myself back to reality each time that it isn't possible nor is this a dream. Even though many days I wish we were all having the same dream?

Comforting her was all I can do as I pray each time for God to take my peace and give it to her. When my children hurt so do I. Being a mom is my favorite blessing but days like these all I want to do is the impossible.

More storms came and I weathered them one by one, some leave scars while others leave bruises. Still going to church when I can but I feel my feet disappearing beneath me as though I was standing in quick sand. Trying to find some time, alone which never happen, guess it wasn't a part of the design plan for my life.

So Christmas was here again and time with family was supposed to be medicine for me but with all that had happened throughout this pass year and the year the boys had pass, a hole was burning within. My dad had also met in an accident that caused me to go back into a dark place, for I didn't get to hug him nor say goodbye on my last visit there. So guilt consumed me, my head swirl with all the, what if's?

Then to add wood to the already burning fire my baby Tyler had suffered injuries due to an accident. Thinking I could handle all this but I was wrong. It didn't happen immediately but after he was release from the hospital, not even words I could speak.

This time I was so lost no one could help for I didn't even have the strength or energy to cry out for help. A week and some pass me by before I realize I am paralyzed. Looking at the date for I had to make arrangement for my newest blessing, my god baby. It was then I realize that the world was going on without me.

I started crying out to the Lord in silent, "I don't like this place, it's too dark."

Break through was way pass needed in this moment.

"Teach me so I can move on Lord, teach me!"

The lesson wasn't coming as soon as I needed it but as always I press on. Having so much to do but still no utterance to move I be consumed with frustration and feeling trapped. For if you know me you know, I hate having things to do!

It's the silliest thing to me at times but to get things done and out the way is one of my many quirks.

So I set aside all things for my baby was on the way, this was nothing new to me for I still got my hidden storage bin. In full gear I went with preparation to the coming of my newest little blessing.

Distractions set in for it was from that to doing stuff for Amarii and Neisha to Shaniece, and getting ready for a conference workshop that I was to be a part of. Still back to my old habits, which seem to die hard, I was in full gear ready to concur everything else but myself.

GOING FULL SPEED AHEAD

# 15

# Closure

So here I am finish with almost all my distraction, taking care of everyone as usual but still haven't given any thought of self. Feeling all is well for I can't seem to stop smiling for my baby is born and he is growing so lovely. More with each day I'm counting my blessing for I have got Chayce.

Knowledge was soon to bring me back to reality, for I know in order to deal with others you have to first deal with yourself. So I asked Shermika for my notes to the class in which she would have me teach so I can be distracted.

That wasn't the case at all, things are subjected to change and so it did. She required of me to fast for the week of the service, which I believe would have been a breeze. Little did I know this was going to be my turning point, the place in which closure is given me? One which last a lifetime and that would equip me to finish this books and move on to all the other prospect on my long list of things to accomplish.

The journey as begun and I am fasting and praying my way through for this conference, but God had to detoxify me from all those things I have stored up over the years of my life. This trip he had no mercy for He ripped out my storage bin, everything was up rooted. All the pain and sorrow I suppressed, every bad thing anyone has ever done to me was resurrected for me to deal with. Before you know it I was down on my knees weeping for it hurt so bad and I couldn't stop nor quench this process of being up rooted.

In a new place, one I have never been before. Speaking in tongues in a way I never had before. Feeling everything being purged from my system, holding on to my tummy wanting to stop this process for it hurt so much. Not even thinking to myself how much I need this but hating what it takes to be rebirth.

My flesh died on that floor and I didn't quite understand it all but the minute I rise up off the floor I knew I was born again. I was spiritually birthed, not only was everything uprooted, but the storage bin was taken and destroyed; now I can walk into my calling. A teacher was birth in me and though the devil tried in that instant to snatch up my reward, I cast him out with the authority that the Lord has given me.

Look I have given you the authority to trample on serpent and scorpions, and over all the power of the enemy: and nothing shall by any means hurt you. (Luke 10:19 KJV)

His divine power has given us everything we need for a godly life through our knowledge of him who called us by his own glory and goodness. (2Peter 1:3 NIV)

My motivation is as it never been before, everything about me is not different but better. I have the assurance of the Lord that it is so.

I may seem to be boasting too much about the authority given to us by the Lord. But our authority builds you up; it doesn't tear us down. So I will not be ashamed of using my authority.
(2 Corinthians 10:8 New Living Translation 2007)

Now I lead a life of example and as God instructs of me. Believing now more than ever that I can do this and an over comer I truly am for God as made himself visible through me. So His instructions are my way of living, I have a new lease on life.

You must teach these things and encourage the believers to do them. You have the authority to correct them when necessary; so don't let anyone disregard what you say.
(Titus 2:15 New Living Translation 2007)

It was the week of fasting and prayers and my expectation where for the Lord to show up and show out for I knew this was His will being done. Everyday me and God would have our secret moments and time together, praying on end that we are able to live with His will for this conference and that it can't quite be perfected unless He puts His hands on it. To let the spirit of perfection be done and His true Will, be done in His name.

So the moment of truth was becoming more real as I traveled to Florida to do my part in this conference. Teaching a class called, 'Birthing from Pain to Purpose.' Wow… my thoughts at this time of getting the email with the material as to what to do for the class. It became more comprehensible why I had to die on the floor March 16, 2013; my experience was becoming more understandable. Going through that experience help me so much, and also it was visible that all who came needed everything this entire conference had to offer. God divine purpose for this event was on point and met everyone at his or her crossroad.

Destiny was on course; my purpose was made transparent to me. Full of courage and anticipation of the future and what was to come, I applied myself and finally 'Being Strong' was no longer a vision but is being birth.

For the first time since my boys had passed and I had received those wonderful words of encouragement from the woman of God, I was able to read every page again. Knowing in this moment spiritual growth is mine. For the terror of going back to that day was haunting me, one of the next reason this book was unable to get finished.

As I read each page, my heart is filled. Like the very first day those words soothe my heart. Only difference this time I was able to smile at it all, knowing that Gods words were still alive even in this time.

In the beginning was the Word, and the Word was with God, and the Word was God.
(John 1:1 NIV)

There are different kinds of working, but in all of them and in everyone it is the same God at work.
(1 Corinthians 12:6 NIV)

Matthew 19:14: But Jesus said, "Let the little children come to me and do not hinder them, for to such belongs the kingdom of heaven.

Psalm 34:18: The Lord is near to the broken hearted and saved the crushed in spirit.

2Corinthians 1:4: Who comforts us in all our afflictions, so that we may be able to comfort those who are in any affliction, with the comfort with which we ourselves are comforted by God.

2Corinthians 4:16-18: So we do not lose heart. Though our outer self is wasted away, our inner self is being renewed day by day. For this light momentary affliction is prepared for us an eternal weight of glory beyond all comparison, as we look not to the things that are seen but to the things that are unseen. For the things that are seen are transient, but the things that are unseen are eternal.

Deuteronomy 3:8: It is the Lord who gives before you. He will be with you; he will not leave you or forsake you. Do not fear or be dismayed.

Being able to smile this time was different for no residue was left behind like the first time I read of these words. God had rewired me and thankful I am for the work He is doing in me.

Sharing on my fan page on Facebook, Gods work in my life. Phone rang and the test of trial was here to rear its ugly head but was snatch down quickly. What I have come away from this experience with is, I can do all things through

Christ Jesus that strengthened me. The garbage bin was truly removed for when trouble arises I had nowhere to store nothing, so I had to deal with it there and then!

April 1, 2013, as I type this final chapter this book comes alive. God as bring closure and understanding to my life. Being able to see His will first hand I am grateful. As I'm writing I am being tested, proving that everything is as it is to be. The truth is being reveal as I come to the end of this book.

As always trial makes its presence known and I have to deal with something I hate having to do, the welfare of my daughter, Shaniece. Wanting the completion of this case to be over with once and for all. This way we can move on with our lives and the fear of losing her can be buried for good.

Believing this the only way, when court issues come to an end but God awaken me through a trial.

So the phone rang and fear set in but there was nowhere to store it so I had to deal with it!

With the phone by my ear till it self-disconnect, I'm lost for words and hurt but it all fell through for the storage bin was ripped out and demolished.

So what now?

Lying in bed, thinking about how to sort through my feelings. A peace and comfort fell upon me, knowing in this minute I needed to call my sis Shermika, why? I don't know.

She answered while I am praying in my mind, that if she did that means she holds the key to the end of this puzzle.

At work but as always she makes time for her little sis. Telling her my need to vent as I went on and on and on, seeking for an answer to why God directed me to her? The words entered my ear and peace flow in.

"Today?" She says.

Light bulb lit up in my mind…

"Just two days before," she continued.

"I know," my respond to her.

At this time my growing strength in the Lord was seeing by me for the first time. I am one to never think about myself or to see the good in me, if it feels right I do it and leave it there. Seeking recognition in my mind is taking from God so I don't think about the things I do good.

Its two days before the two years of my boys' death. We both gave off a wow impression...

"I know sis this always happen, it's either the first of the month or the last of the month before, always asking Shayne why?"

Seeking God during these pass twenty-three months as to why this always happened but this time I knew and was able to deal with it. God has been taking care of me this whole journey and now I have the assurance that these things never came to break me but to build me up for the glory of the Lord.

I have come into the world as a light, so that no one who believes in me should stay in darkness. (John 12:46 NIV)

Consider it pure joy, my brothers and sisters, whenever you face trials of many kinds. (James 1:2)

With this in my heart it was clear that this too would pass. It's evident that I have grown through my experience and was ready to be a blessing to others through my testimonies.

There was more to come, which will give me confirmation that I'm on the right path. My daughter came into the room and said, "Mommy I really miss my brothers and wish they were here in the flesh, real mommy, just like me."

"Honey me too, but you have them with you always they are your angels and will always look out for you."

The look in her face wasn't one that any mother would like to see but the spirit stepped in that instant and redirected my thoughts. It was so instant and different from all the other times that I've looked in her eyes and seen this pain. Difference this time, for the first it was visible to me that my baby needed help, more than I could offer her, so I begin thanking God for provision to do so.

God as done an amazing work in my princess and being mommy truth is we want to do it all but can't. So my next assignment is to continue helping my daughter but getting her additional support that will help her heal for her future requires it. She deserves a full life and that she will have, one fill with potential and opportunities that will take her where she needs to be. The foundation I have built with the guidance of the Lord, so it's time to do what's best for my gem Shaniece.

Before I could finish that thought, typing away the phone rang and it was my lawyer again but serenity was mine. Tearing down all strongholds, the enemy as developed a new way to block the success of this book. Today I stand boldly, declaring that 'Being Strong' as been born and nothing will cripple its destiny. Going full force into the future with my newest blessing from God, 'Being Strong.'

Do not be anxious about anything, but in every situation, by prayer and petition, with thanksgiving, present your requests to God. 7 And the peace of God, which transcends all understanding, will guard your heart and your minds in Christ Jesus. (Philippians 4:6-7 NIV)

The Start of a New...

# Bonus Chapter

Life is a journey, but its one that isn't worth living if you learnt nothing. I must say the past almost four year have been an experience of a lifetime. So many things have been revealed unto me, and endless lessons have I learnt. Could I have imagined this would have been my outcome, I dare not say yes. From my story you have some idea of my testimony, but I have decided to share my journey since the publishing of this book in eBook. Sharing also something's that had been holding me back from my purpose, which have been waiting on me to catch up to it. Therefore I decided to do this bonus chapter for the printed version of 'Being Strong.'

Life is my new obsession, it amaze me the amount of years I been alive, yet its just this season of my existence that my desires and I have become one. I am alive for the first in my lifetime. Truth is told, my life I took for granted. Everyday was another day, week, month year. I am thankful however for it added up to mountain of experience and cause me to savor every second of each waking day of my life.

Would I say life would have been better if none of these things ever happened? Hmmm...as much as it wasn't easy, truth is I wouldn't change anything. Will I ever stop missing my boys or feel empty because they not around, counting and celebrating their birthday, wondering who they would be that day or time in life if only they where still here with me. That I can answer boldly, Never! I know with God all things are possible but my gut tells me He require me to have these feelings for it makes a better me. It's like a tune up to a car, its necessary for it to keep running smooth. These moments motivate, encourage, strengthen, build me up and keep me from wavering in my relation with Christ.

My thoughts in regard to my experiences are never negative. My life is fill with joy and peace, an inconceivable amount of it. What this does for me is cause me to live a full life and be a blessing to those I come in contact with. This could be different on the flip side but it comes down to choices. For me, I chose to live! Why? I do it not for self but for all those who hurt because of similar circumstances as myself. Hope, that's my desire. This is what I chose to give to others through my story. Moments do come when I miss them but it doesn't break me. For all that I'm able to overcome is through Christ who strengthens me. Thank you isn't enough; this is why I dedicate everyday of my life to He who gives life.

Throughout my life it was made possible for me to overcome molestation, emotional and mental abuse, not only from others but also from self and the loss of my sons. I will share a little about the custody battle for my only birth daughter, my divorce case and learning to let go and let God. There is many more obstacle but I will have to save that for another book, laugh out loud. I would be writing for days.

As a child I remember my innocence fighting to detach itself from me. As I am writing it dawn on me, you maybe wondering why share? Why now? Well as I said in the beginning of this chapter on this journey, many things I have learn. Through these lessons it become visible to me that once you have overcome you can say what you been through for deliverance is in effect.

How many know the hand of God is always on you? Living testimony I am. Fighting within as to why this all happened. It was 1988, the year my father pass away. One I had trusted violated my body. What that did is make it much harder for me to process. Especially at the age of seven you have no clue as to what to do or say therefore silence was my thought of action. Many years and I said nothing to anyone that could help me that is. Confided in my age group, one I explain it as though it was a dream, then another the complete step by step process for I knew she wouldn't say it back and she didn't until things got out of hand years later. Yes I'm a secretive person, so that was a challenge for me. Today I share with everyone who picks up this book for there is a need to share which I cant quench.

It took years to come to grip with what had happen, for the very reason that is norm to us as human being. It was my belief that it was possible and within my ability to fix it. It's that instinctive feel, a gut feeling of some sort that teaches that it's otherwise. From experience its known to be impossible. Why? Believe it or not, it's the truth;

only God can make us whole. Once I made the decision to surrender it was visible to me that I had mastered how to patch up emotional wounds. When expose to the love of God clarification of restoration becomes a language you understand. It's only through His love that healing begins and loving self becomes natural.

The love felt is like none experienced throughout my life. Have you experience the love of God then this feeling is no secret to you. This feeling for those who haven't experience it, it's an indescribable feeling, believe me. You must notice that it is so, for I can't even explain it to you, I just know it is. Just know this, you will never be the same and that's a great thing. You'll be experiencing the ultimate you for He is within you. This is why I'm sharing this part of my journey, for with His love we begin to do above our self. You begin to work for the kingdom. It's my greatest desire to help others be free from self; I have been delivered for I trust the process. The shades are down and I'm stripped down to my true identity. Yes, the mask has been removed and I'm baring it all for deliverance is mine. I am set free from my self!

Growing up with this while dealing with the death of my father was more than any little girl should have to deal with. My job at that age was to be carefree. Be a child! It's evident that it leads to the path chosen. This made me hurt myself, not physically but to settle was norm. Mediocre was acceptable at that point in my life. Somehow the 'me' I knew not yet, was in battle with what was thought and seen as I grew up. I believe that was the move of God in me, it just wasn't relatable to me.

Growing up it says children live what they learn and at time this mentality learnt from ethnicity mold our belief mechanism. Therefore instead of saying I have been abuse, we dissect the why it wasn't physical but psychological and mental abuse is the description of ones abusive relationship. It happened only once and I fought back so to my belief we had a disagreement and I fought back so it wasn't abuse. Due to my reality I fought back, throw a punch here and there, so that word abuse didn't describe my relationship.

See the result of that lack of the 'Agape' love. If received, loving myself would be priority. A language understood, preventing me from accepting that treatment or giving it, calling it equal or getting even. You see how love reveals even self. Looking in the mirror and not only seeing what been done to me but facing the fact of what I have done to someone else and self. The reflection of self is the opposite of who God call me to BE. It became visible to me that something's identified in others is visible for the same attributes are acquired in self. Its always-in ones best interest to look inward.

Though those on the outside would classify me as an ideal wife. There were moments when I would loose myself to get my point across. In the depth of my inner core something kept pulling at me. It was known that I deserve better and should not settle but the battle of who I was and who I am call to be, battled for 'the crown.' Again background had a lot to do with what one believe, so my advise to you is to create a new for your generation to come. That's my goal when it comes to my children and family. To not be statistic but to be unique for we are wonderfully made and they need to see that. Therefore find your identity and impart it into your love ones. We are children of the living God, so our DNA is more than skin color, nationality and our surname. Our core value is found only in Him!

It was thought that to be a good wife was to wash, cook, clean and care for the children. Therefore when the need to have a voice surface it wasn't normal or accepted. In my world that wasn't acceptable! That belief of saying nothing wasn't in my mechanism, therefore in my world that just wasn't going to work for me. So we clashed a lot. Especially after all the cheating, disrespect and disgrace. It's said that people can do unto you what you allow them to. So I stuck with it for all the wrong reasons. Truth is told I wanted that fairytale; so sharing myself with someone new was out of the question. Also his feelings mattered and our children were the highlight of all my choices.

It amazes me even till this day that things went the way they did. Somewhat that is! It took us four years of being together to even have our first argument. My belief was based on, it started so well therefore it would end well and things will forever remain the same but my eyes opened when I got saved. That's when it became clear as to why. We were different individuals with completely opposite desires and destination. Let me not forget to clarify a few things before I continue. Having a voice is necessary but there is also a right way to talk to another, whether it is your spouse, friend, family or child/ren. What you dish out will definitely come back to you so show love and listening for directions regarding your relationships' this way you know when to walk away and when to stay put.

What I have learnt is that God will give you double for your troubles. Though He never sent you wherever you ended up He will provide a way out. One that will redeem you! We shouldn't rely on what God will do when we get ourselves in these messes but learn this day and be useable to the Kingdom.

Double for my trouble, is God opening my heart once again. Still a little inner battle going on but its known just a little opening is all it takes, right? Its been almost five year of separation and three years of being legally divorce and the truth is I never see myself getting marry to begin with much less to be thinking about doing it again. With God this is no way impossible, for if it's His will I'm up for it. Why? I failed the last time around not God. My heart is somewhat more receptive this time around, for closure and healing came. Again that is the hands of God in my life. You know what they say about love, it moves mountains!

Throughout the accident, custody/divorce battle, bitter was I. Telling all sides of me is important! Admitting you were wrong is key to being delivered. I believe he was selfish for all he had done to me in the pass. Keyword "pass"! Lesson learnt that was then and this is now and the power to bring forth change is NOW! Why ever was I taking my pass into my future and it wasn't for encouragement. If ever you decide to keep the pass around make sure it's to motivate you to where you are to be. NOTHING ELSE!

So I took control of my life by turning it over to The Lord. Some maybe tired of hearing about God in my story but I am unapologetic when it comes to my destiny for He is 'the' way. Accept it or not, know this it's the truth and one more try Him then get back to me for you wont be disappointed.

It didn't happen overnight for I couldn't forgive self therefore it was impossible for me to accept that it's okay to forgive him. Truth is forgiving him for cheating, abuse and even the accident came almost immediately after they each happened. After the boys had pass away, my growth was immense. Not by any means over night but all my time with God paid off. Being teachable and receptive made a great difference in my decision making at this time in my life. Keep this in mind; once you overcome one area be prepared for the next battle for it is coming. In this game you have to be on your 'A' game. Don't be saddened by this reality for this is how we build our spiritual muscles. Where we at maybe all good but keep in mind greater is in store than where we choose to settle and call enough for He said, 'He will do exceedingly and abundantly above all we can imagine.' Therefore keep aiming higher and dreaming bigger.

It was his inconsideration toward my pain that made me bitter. How could he? How? Dismay doesn't even describe my feelings then. You'll be surprise that when you believe you are over it you truly aren't. This is where this bonus chapter came from. I can't store anything anymore for God tore out my storage bin therefore confronting things is how my story unfolds since then. Added bonus this also gives me a way to connect with my readers.

Yes I forgave him for the pass for it was behind me even with the cases pending. So I dealt with these cases with a mentality of straight on collision. My patience was stretch thin; keep in mind I don't have much to begin with. Playing with this thought for so long, for my heart dreaded ever having to do it. Let go! This thought I wrestle with for so long. Praying on end for what my mind was telling me to do was about to be the hardest and most unbelievable thing I would ever do.

Deposition came in July 2013, months before my eBook publishing date. It was time to remove her from my heart and memory. Training my heart for months to just let go. Yes its crazy thinking about it now, I was getting ready to let go of my princess forever. Believing in my heart she also died in the accident with the boys. This way my nightmare be over for she wouldn't exist so I can't miss what I didn't have since the accident. He would stop coming after me using Shaniece as an excuse to keep torturing me.

My belief at that time was if he loved her he would let her be. It's not as though she knew him or should I say remembered him. The time spent in her life was not much for it was a bit of her new born and toddler years not consecutive. She was only four by the time the boys passed away and was still alive because I made a choice to send her to be with my brother. Otherwise my reality would be that which I coach myself to believe. My three birth children would be dead! Maybe I was being selfish for he deserve to know her and or her to know him but I was protecting my child. Doing what I believe to be best for her, especially all that news would probably set back all the work put in. She was dealing with the boys' death and missing her sisters and that was more than she needed to be dealing with in my mind. Never wanted her to loose that feeling of innocence as I did.

It been two years and I have not yet breathe. From I got the news that my sons pass away it been one thing after the next. It was as though they were set in motion even before one could pass. No breathing room to deal with what had really happen. I survive because God was carrying me from day one, but my heart hunger to feel. It was expected with such tragedy so I wanted to be normal. This is why this plan was necessary for I wanted closure. He wasn't for me and this was known to me. Giving him what he illustrated he wanted seeing it was said to be the purpose for his action. It was a set up from the heaven that is evident. When you are ready to give up that said thing and more God is getting ready to bless you with. Unknowingly I was walking into my overflow.

Back to my decision... My intention was to sign my daughter over to him. Relinquishing all rights, this way no phone calls, no relationship, no nothing! I had been working on my emotion, this way once its final I will be able to live without regrets. This decision my lawyer didn't agree to but my mind was made up. She thought it was in my best interest to get him to settle out of court. Not sure as to how this would be possible for I was set in my own ways not believing I should. My heart was overwhelmed by this time. God saw this and lifted the burden. He reached out to me. Why? No idea!

The phone rang out to voicemail, so calling my lawyer was my reaction. She suggested that talking to him would be in my best interest. Hesitated to do so, but eventually I did. She wanted this in hope of settling for it was better than my idea in her sight, especially for Shaniece. Truth be told, enough was enough! There was no room for uncertainty.

Speaking to him as suggested by my lawyer and relating each conversation to her. Yes, my stubborn self took her advise. We settled out of court and the treasures that came with this were being able to love on my girls. This was no longer a dream but our reality. In order for Shaniece to get comfortable enough to talk with him, I had to show trust. She emulates her mommy, yes she does. In her eyes I am wise and exemplary. So showing her he can be trusted she warm up to having conversations with him. Is name became one that was learnt and welcome into out lives.

Before the warm up came, that very summer holiday of 2013 she was able to spend summer with Abigail, which aid the process. They were both overjoyed we had tons of fun. Being a mother brings much joy to my life, guess that's why I have inherited so many children over my lifetime. I am up to eleven godchildren and counting. Not to mention I am a grandmother for my children inherited decided to crown me with this title. You can just imagine how I felt being able to run ward again. As my girls slept I watch them nightly, giving God thanks for them and this blessed possibility Christmas 2013.

Did I imagine this would be my reward once I took myself out the equation or should I say my feeling? The transformation continues not just growth but a new level of appreciation for the process. Obedience pays, stubborn me have learnt that on this journey of finding self. Before I get to the other side of this blessing I'm going to skip to 2014. We sat at the grave, myself, Olivia and Abigail. Imagining Shayne smiling for it's all over.

My limited mind would say for the fight for Shaniece is over but my develop self, know it's greater. It's seeing he didn't die in vain so I keep living their legacy.

My girls make me smile, proud is minimal to how they make me feel. It's discernible that they are broken some. From stories we share with each other, its evident God been with them through it all and they felt it. Shaniece said it and it was so! Though it seem bad to be broken in the eyes of the world; it's necessary in the spiritual to be broken this way one can be made whole. Worried not for I give my children over to God and live an admirable life so they have an idea of what happens when you serve The Lord wholeheartedly.

You get the idea; I'm beyond joyful of the turn out. A little too comfortable I got for growth is possible for all so I poured the love of God unto him. It didn't work for timing is Gods not mine. This time around it doesn't affect me for knowledge is mine. It will be one day but in God time he will be the ideal father I want for my girls. So behind the scene I keep praying him up for prayer bring forth growth, each in its own timing.

We communicate when necessary for we share children. We are very modest towards each other in and out of the sight of our children. Am I please with the outcome? Yes, for greater days are ahead! He is accustom to me being there for him always and is very much dependent. My fault?

Somewhat! Experience teaches me how to do this in moderation, which is ideal for where I am now and to come. What I take away from this experience? Balance!

All in all I am a winner. Surprised? No, I serve an infinite God. Winning is an expectation in my life. This journey came with many lessons and I am thankful for them all. Through all the praying moments, braking and pressing my identity been discovered. Eternal gratitude is what I have today!

One thing distinguishable through my experiences is, we all have a purpose. Thankfully I found mine; therefore I'm open to all that the future holds for my life. Can I say what they all are? No! One fact, I am ready to face the world and embrace each as they become visible to me.

The Beginning...

# Author

Stacey Ann Satchell is a woman after Gods heart. She lives for the Lord, her children, family, and helping others. She shares her story so she can become a blessing to those going through life struggles or for those who need a purpose to keep moving forward. Her desires are to help those in need and hurting from their daily battles. She is the owner of 'Wrap Me In Your Arms Inc', Founded in April 2011 in South Florida. It's created to uplift others, with hopes of helping single mothers and donate car seats to those who can't afford it. Also to join force with other organizations to uplifts and helps others. You can stay posted on upcoming events at www.wrapmeinyourarmsinc.com or like us on Facebook www.facebook.com/wrapmeinyourarms (feel free to leave your testimony or request prayer)

# Contact Information

Company Name: Stacey Ann Satchell
Author: Stacey Ann Satchell
Address: New York, NY

My Websites:
www.staceyannsatchell.com
www.wrapmeinyourarmsinc.com

Email: staceyann.n.satchell@gmail.com

Twitter: www.twitter.com/Stacey_Satchell
Facebook:
www.facebook.com/StaceyAnnSatchell

Instagram:
www.instagram.com/Staceyann_Satchell

www.ingramcontent.com/pod-product-compliance
Lightning Source LLC
Chambersburg PA
CBHW071700090426
42738CB00009B/1602